TEACHING GREATNESS

Teaching Greatness

The MOLE Theory

**DR. NORMAN R. JOHNSON &
ANGELA E. MORIARITY, PHD**

MOLE Theory, LLC

Dedicated to Brenda J. Johnson,
a businesswoman who mastered the ability to uphold high standards
yet be supportive at the same time. She challenges everyone to work at
their highest level every day. She is a woman who makes our lives easier.

CONTENTS

Dedication	iv
Preface	1

BECOMING A MOLE

1	Leading Yourself	8
2	Communication and the MOLE	23
3	Execution and the MOLE	58
4	Tools, Tips, and Techniques for a MOLE	69

MOLE LEADERSHIP

5	The MOLE Leader	90
6	Personality Factors for the MOLE Leader	96
7	Motivational Factors for the MOLE Leader	100

8	Company Culture	103
9	Hiring the MOLE	110
10	Training the MOLE	130
11	Mentoring for the MOLE	150
12	Coaching for the MOLE	158
13	Monitoring as a MOLE Leader	170
14	Strategic Planning for the MOLE Leader	178
15	Recognizing the MOLE	195
16	Compensating the MOLE	210
17	Tools, Tips, and Techniques for the MOLE Leader	216

MOLD

18	People Who Make Our Lives Difficult	232
	Closing	253
	About The Authors	255
	Suggested Reading List	257

Index 258

Copyright © 2023 by Dr. Norman R. Johnson and Angela E. Moriarity, PhD.

All rights reserved. No part of this book may be reproduced in any manner whatsoever without written permission except in the case of brief quotations embodied in critical articles and reviews. This book is protected under the copyright laws of the United States and other countries throughout the world. Country of first publication: United States of America. Any unauthorized exhibition, distribution, or copying of this book or any part thereof (including website, webinars, trainings, etc.) may result in civil liability and criminal prosecution.

All brand names and product names used in this book are trade names, service marks, trademarks and registered trademarks of their respective owners. The publishers and the book are not associated with any product or vendor mentioned in this book. None of the companies referenced within the book have endorsed the book.

 The stories, all names, characters, and incidents written may have started from memory and consistently took a fictitious, inaccurate, and dramatic turn. No identification with actual persons (living or deceased), places, buildings, and products is intended or should be inferred and would only be coincidental. In short, everything is made up, but the issues are real- focus on the concepts.

First edition
Editing by Brittany Krysinski
Illustration by Mike Sofka

First Printing, 2023

Preface

Consider the following three questions:

Is your life perfect?
Why not?
What have you done about it?

This book discusses a new way of thinking about leadership; a new tool to apply to decision-making, the training of your staff, and to your decisions about work-life balance. It is based on the philosophy airline attendants tell passengers: if oxygen masks come down, we must take care of ourselves first. The theory is before you can take care of other people, you must take care of yourself. This is as true in life as it is on an airplane. Certainly, it follows that this is true in leadership. Before you can be a great leader, your life must be as organized and as perfect as you can make it.

In 2002, Dr. Johnson and his wife Brenda started a business called Advanced Correctional Healthcare, Inc. The purpose of the company was to provide health care to an underserved portion of the population: the incarcerated patient. They developed systems of health care delivery including hiring doctors and nurses, providing medications, handling hospitalizations, utilizations, and even third-party administration for payment of bills. The programs were individually designed to help each sheriff and jail administration solve the problems they had to deal with daily. In order to accomplish this, they had to become experts in correctional health care, provide training across many states, and nationally improve the overall quality of health care to this underserved population. As the company grew from a dozen employees to hundreds, leadership became an issue.

They preferred to promote from within the company when possible and would often identify an employee who was very smart and hard-working and promote them into a leadership position, only to see them fail miserably. It occurred to them they couldn't expect a person with no leadership experience to do well if they had not provided leadership training. That led to extensive research on the subject of leadership and an aggressive training program instituted throughout the company. True leadership is rare, and is why it is such a big deal when each of us experience it.

The concept of MOLE Theory came later as they began to observe leaders who would become burned out or simply overwhelmed with the volume of decision-making they felt they had to do in order to handle all of their objectives. They began to recommend the individual think about those things that were making their life uncomfortable or more difficult and what together could be done to make those items better. Maybe the individual was on the road too much, and away from home too often. Maybe they had too many phone calls coming in after hours. Whatever the problem was, if the Dr. Johnson and individual sat down together as a group, they could usually figure out a solution that would make the situation better. Sometimes it took quite a while to fix the more difficult issues, but at least they could see the light at the end of the tunnel. Everyone knew the situation would be resolved.

The concept of MOLE Theory became stronger as we continued to promote individually thinking about ourselves and what was necessary to make each of our lives easier. One of the first things identified is before you can become a great leader, your life must be organized and as perfect as you can make it.

The concept of MOLE Theory—**M**aking **O**ur **L**ives **E**asier—may at first be a little difficult to understand. There will be those who will confuse it with personal greed—doing things to make your life easier at the expense of other people. With a little consideration, we believe you will quickly see it is not in your long-term best interest to be greedy, cut corners, or take advantage of other people. While you may appear to gain short-term benefit, the long-term consequences would be negative, not in your best interest, and would not make your life easier.

MOLE Theory is based upon the concept that leaders are not doers. They do not do their employees' work for them. Leaders are responsible for organizing a team of employees to accomplish a specific goal. This includes hiring the right people, training, mentoring, monitoring, recognizing, and when necessary, disciplining. Finally, when you find a person who truly makes your life easier, identify what they are worth and what their compensation should include.

Before your life can be made easier, all the aspects of your job and your areas of responsibility—which may include a department or a company—must be running smoothly and at peak performance. When things are perfect, life is easier. The question becomes, what is preventing your life from being easier? This gets us back to the three questions. Is your business life and your staff perfect? If not, why not? Finally, what have you done to improve the situation? By constantly looking at yourself and identifying the areas of your responsibility with which you are unhappy, you will identify those areas causing you the most stress. This will allow you to define what areas you need to focus on with training, new programs, or at times replacing certain employees who are MOLD—**M**aking **O**ur **L**ives **D**ifficult—and cannot be improved.

MOLE Theory is a system of thinking about personal productivity and leadership. This is quite different from the way you have been trained. In this system you are constantly testing your gut to see how you feel about the way things are going, how you react and respond to trouble, and how you structure areas of correction and improvement. You as the leader clearly understand the work that must be done. Therefore, you are the best judge of what is working and not working; what is stressing you and making you feel better about the job. Your gut does not lie to you, and when it makes you feel uncomfortable, something must be done to improve the situation.

MOLE Theory is all about you. If you are to have a perfect experience at work, all your direct reports must be perfect and they must have a perfect experience at work. This requires you to assist them in reviewing their direct reports, to look at their responsibilities, and constantly determine how they can make things better for themselves. How could things run more smoothly? It is highly unlikely they have ever thought purely of making their own life easier. Going forward, it will be your job to not only think in these patterns for yourself, but to help your direct reports to think that way as well.

This book is divided into three sections. The first section is designed to help you personally develop the skills and attributes of a MOLE employee—someone who always makes their boss' life easier while making their own life easier at the same time. In this section you will find chapters on communication, execution, and techniques you can learn and teach to other employees. Section two is about becoming a MOLE leader. It is designed to help you identify and hire MOLE employees. Included in section two are chapters on training, mentoring, and coaching. Section three deals with MOLD. It describes the problem with people who do not perform and teaches techniques to resolve the situation including discipline and/or removing the employee.

Throughout the book, we share stories of our successes and challenges, and you will have an opportunity to meet many new animals, as well as viruses and zombies. It all comes down to the most important creature of all: the MOLE. When your direct reports are all MOLEs, suddenly your life becomes easier.

We hope you will be able to use this book as a personal guide or roadmap to develop those personal skills you need to become a MOLE employee and to pass them on to those people that work for you in order to make your life easier. Therefore, the entire purpose of this book is to assist you in gaining those skills necessary to guide your staff to do the right thing, at the right time, and in the right place.

A Note About Pearls

As you progress through this book, you will notice chapter pearls being listed at the end. Pearls are thought to enhance integrity and advance wisdom along a journey toward perfection. The items listed are selected as the items which will enhance your own integrity and wisdom as you progress through the book. Take some time, go back and ensure you understand the topics. Ensure you fully understand the pearls before you accept them. Each chapter's pearls could hypothetically be placed on a neckless. By the end of the book you would have a full string of pearls to complete the fine jewelry piece.

BECOMING A MOLE

| 1 |

Leading Yourself

There are three levels of MOLE leadership. Level one is leading yourself. Level two is becoming a team leader. Level three is becoming an advanced leader. This section focuses on level one, leading yourself. Before you can be a great leader of people, you must learn to lead yourself. You must develop those qualities of character so all people who work with you can see your professionalism, integrity, and moral compass. You must personally perform your duties at a level that makes your superiors' lives easier. MOLE employees have learned the abilities of great communication, complete execution of their duties, and composure under stress. When they have a problem that must be presented to their supervisor, they always bring a solution or a recommendation. When you have achieved these things, you will truly be on the road to becoming a MOLE.

The Airline Attendant

MOLE leadership means thinking about what is in your own best interest and what things can make your life easier, and then using your gut to tell you what is right or wrong. It is the basic philosophy of taking care of yourself so you can take care of other people. We try to pick up basic philosophy anywhere we can. One of the best philosophers is the airline attendant. The attendant says, if we lose pressure and the oxygen mask comes down, you must take that mask and put it on yourself first before you put it on your two-year-old child. Why is that? Do you not want to sacrifice yourself for your child? The answer is an emphatic no. You must take care of yourself first. If something were to happen to you, then your child would be left to fend for themself. Once you are okay, you can take care of other people. This is true on an airplane and it is true in life. If you think you are sacrificing yourself for your husband, your family, for anything, you are not going to survive. The marriage is not going to survive. The kids are not going to thrive. You are going to have troubled children. Always take care of yourself first and make sure your needs are met, then you will be able to take care of everyone else. That is the first thing you have to think about.

Your moral compass is vital. We have known employees who were brilliant and bonded well with their clients, but once they got off the job their moral compass was so low it became apparent to all those who worked around them. Their coworkers began to think less of them. Eventually it was clear they did not demonstrate our value system and the values of those we wish to be around. In our company, 360 surveys are done on all leadership positions. The 360 survey is a series of questions based upon our values that are answered by 7-10 people who work directly with the leader. This gives us an overall view of how the individual matches our company culture. For many leaders, the scores from their colleagues eventually fall so low that they feel they have to move on because they are no longer a good cultural fit for the company. They have lost the respect of their peers. When you look back, their moral compass caused the problem.

How do you become a MOLE? In order to be a MOLE, you have to be a good person. You have to have the personal qualities of a good person. There are certain commonalities about good people with which we all relate. This turns out to be key in leadership. As we continued to look at this concept of a good person, we realized that to be a good leader and a good person you have to be a happy person. You cannot be grumpy. It turns out that when you really study happiness there are certain things you must have. You must have them in the quantity and quality you need them.

Six Areas of Life

Overall, the six areas of life a MOLE must have organized are:

1. Health
2. Personal Philosophy/Spirituality
3. Environment
4. Money
5. Career/Work
6. Love

These are not in any particular order. They are all critical because if any area is not completely organized to your satisfaction you will not be happy. We usually think of this in the form of a hand, because it helps us remember what areas we must focus on at any given time.

Health

The first finger is the thumb, which is your health. You must have the very best health possible for you. This does not mean you have to be absolutely disease free or that you cannot be happy if you have diabetes, hypertension, or even cancer. What it does mean is that whatever health issues you have, you should have them under the best control possible. You are working to maintain the highest level of health you possibly can.

If you have diabetes, follow your diet, take your medication, check your blood sugar, look at your hemoglobin A1C's periodically, and see your doctor on a regular basis for updates. If you have cancer, follow your doctor's orders. Be involved with the treatment decisions. This has been studied many times and always shows people who are in control of their treatments feel better, are happier, and the outcomes are actually better.

Make sure you have a personal plan for health maintenance. How should you eat? How should you exercise? How much rest do you get? It is important to keep daily records of your progress on health-related goals. For example, note how much exercise you got, if you met your goals, and how many calories you ate for the day. Any areas where you did not meet your goals must be made up in the next day or two. The key point is that a MOLE has and lives a plan.

Personal Philosophy/Spirituality

Number two is your index finder, your pointing finger, the finger that gives you direction, your personal philosophy or spirituality. It really does not matter what your personal philosophy is as long as you don't violate it. It needs to support you. It needs to work well for you. We worked with a young lady who was quite good; she was very smart, but part of her personal philosophy was that she and her husband had what they called an "open marriage". To them, this meant they could have relations with other people outside of marriage. They both agreed and they never fought over the issue. It was their personal philosophy and lifestyle. Over a period of time, these relationships got in the way of her job and her marriage. She lost her job and lost her marriage. We suggest this was not a personal philosophy that served her well. At other times, we have seen people who considered themselves "good family men", and yet they would spend most of their time in a tavern drinking with their friends and spending far more money than they should.

The rule here is MOLEs think about their philosophy, work on their philosophy, believe their philosophy, and live it day in and day out. When a MOLE violates their personal philosophy, they are lying to themselves and violating their own rules.

Environment

The third finger, the middle finger, is your environment. You must have the right environment to be happy. It means you need to live in the right type of house or apartment, wear the kind of clothes that make you comfortable and proud, drive the right kind of car, and when you travel you stay in comfortable hotels.

We have traveled with very wealthy people who would spend no money at all on hotels because to them "it's just a place to sleep". In fact, they were very uncomfortable while they were in the room. In his personal life, Dr. Johnson has traveled with friends to various locations. Once, a friend requested to book everyone's hotel for an upcoming trip. The day of the trip came and when the group arrived at the hotel, they were met with a hotel staff member who was drunk. The staff member was too unsteady to assist with luggage, got lost showing the group to their rooms, and finally placed Dr. Johnson in a dirty room with broken locks. Dr. Johnson spent the night with a chair propped against the handle of the door, wondering how he ended up in an environment he did not feel safe or comfortable with. Always consider your environment. Make sure it is something that is comfortable and nurturing to you.

If you come into our corporate office, you will notice very quickly we live this philosophy throughout the entire building. The offices and training areas are attractive, and nice pieces of artwork decorate the walls and shelves. All of this is meant to make the work environment more pleasant and comfortable.

The corporate philosophy we try to practice throughout the company is to always hire and work with "nice" people. These are people who are pleasant to work with, do not raise their voices, and do not get in people's faces. On more than one occasion we have had employees tell us we are wrong and there are times you must yell at people and raise your voice to get them to do the right thing. We simply disagree, and when talking doesn't work, we tend to remove those people from a leadership role. It is our corporate philosophy that there is no place for that kind of behavior. It creates a bad environment.

We have had leaders who as part of their job had a car supplied to them by the company. Occasionally we looked at a car and found it was dirty and unkempt. The car was littered with disorganized work papers and even had fast food wrappers lying on the backseat and floor. Always keep your area clean and organized, it will simplify your life. Clutter in any area puts stress on you. MOLEs have a habit of decluttering their work area and their life.

Money

The fourth finger is your ring finger, and this signifies money. Everyone has a set point for money—the amount of money you believe you are worth. One of Dr. Johnson's very first set points was $3 an hour. That was massively more than he was making at the time, but this was many years ago. Over time your set point will change. Today, he believes he is worth more than $3 an hour. A detailed account of money management is beyond the realm of this book. It is important you understand what you believe you are worth and you are being paid what you are worth. Your expectations must be realistic and they must be market driven. This means you cannot believe you are worth $150,000 a year if everybody in the marketplace is doing the same job you do for $70,000 a year. On the other hand, it is vital you continue to constantly improve your knowledge and skillset going forward. People always think they are worth more money simply because they have added more years to the time they have worked for a company. That really is not true. All they are entitled to if they are doing the same job with no new skills is a cost of living increase. Your business needs people who are more and more valuable. In order to do this, you must constantly train yourself forward. MOLEs pick up new skills and develop new abilities that are more valuable to the company. This will come back to you in the form of more money and higher productivity.

Career/Work

The fifth finger, the little finger, signifies career and work. If you are to be happy, you have to have a career you are proud of, that gives you the recognition you desire, as well as the money you want. People have had jobs they simply were not proud of working. Because of that, they were constantly looking to move on to something else. It is generally a bad idea to go from one career field to an entirely new career or field where you have to go back and start at the beginning. Always try to build on your existing skill set.

While not impossible to do, switching to an entirely new career or field takes a lot of time, money, and effort. Both Dr. Johnson and Dr.

Moriarity have experience with this. Dr. Johnson started in the career field of manufacturing, a trade he learned from a young age. It was not until later in his life that he and his wife realized the career path he was on was not bringing him joy or going to help them meet their future goals. Therefore, his wife worked up to three jobs simultaneously while Dr. Johnson focused on changing his career track to the medical field. Because of his wife's support and their focus on achieving their goals, the Johnsons were able to surpass their former goals. Dr. Moriarity's husband was on an accounting career path out of college, but ultimately did not find it to be a good fit for his active lifestyle. The two planned a change together, and Dr. Moriarity worked full time while her husband went back to school in a new field. In both scenarios, a more difficult path was taken and it took more time than building on a current skill set. Ideally, if you are in a field you enjoy and can see a future in, you can add value to your experience and company by growing in your same skill set to meet your future goals.

There are two basic ways MOLEs can expand their value for a company. One is simply to work harder. Hard work should always be a given in any position you take. Two is to expand their knowledge base through further education and training. The best way to grow is through further training, education, going to college, taking courses, or whatever you can do to further your personal career. Check with your human resources department to see if there are programs that will help pay for certain training that may be of benefit to the company. Most departments like accounting, human resources, and information technology have many new certifications that can be obtained through further study and testing. Most of these will make you more valuable to your company. Work with your human resources department and try to design a career path that allows for financial growth for yourself if the company does not automatically do that.

For talented people in the company, one of the most important benefits is professional growth through promotions. A MOLE who wishes to grow through promotions must be able to see and believe that if they stay with a company long enough, they will have a fair chance to be promoted into positions above them. They need to see the company is growing, expanding, and that positions will open up.

Love

The sixth element is signified by the palm of your hand. Your palm draws all the other fingers together—love. You have got to have adequate amounts of love. That means all the different kinds of love, from married love to love for a pet, children, parents, and friends. The key here is to actually consider and have a plan for nourishing the relationships you have in your life. If you take them for granted and do not tend to them on a regular basis, you will have trouble. You can't neglect your significant other, your children, your pets, friends, or any aspect of your relationships without problems developing. You will never be able to be happy unless you are completely fulfilled in the area of love.

The Gardens of Your Life

These six areas are like six gardens of your life. If you do not tend to these six areas constantly, weeds will start to grow. The minute you believe you have one area of your life totally controlled and you do not have to think about it anymore, trouble will develop. Maybe you just bought a new house. It is the perfect house, everything in it is perfect, and so you do not give it another thought. But before long, the pipes are leaking and the house needs to be painted again. Trouble is developing. You must constantly focus on each of the six areas of your life and constantly have a plan to update and improve all six gardens of your life. Once you have these areas controlled, you will be a happy person. You will be content, comfortable, and you will be prepared to live your core values. You will meet all the criteria of what we call "a good person". You will have learned how to lead yourself.

Now that you understand the six basic areas you must have organized in order to be happy, the question is what do you do with this information? How do you implement this? The answer is that a MOLE has a personal strategic plan for happiness.

Strategic Plan for Happiness

In this strategic plan, you will write down a minimum of at least one goal for each of the six areas in the gardens of your life. To begin the process, think about how you want your life to be organized five years from now. How healthy will you be? What is your personal philosophy, and will you be living it? How will your environment be organized? What kind of car will you drive? What type of home will you live in? How much money will you be earning? How will your work or career be organized, and what will you be doing five years from now? Finally, how will the area of love be organized in your life? Will you be married, will you have pets, will you have children? All of these things must be considered before you start, and you must think five years ahead. When you have a clear view of that, you now write goals for one year. The goals must be time specific and easily measurable.

The first area is health. There are many aspects of your health you could write goals for. An easy one is if you determine you would like to lose 12 pounds over the next year. Your goal would be, "I will lose one pound a month for the next 12 months." This is a goal that you can easily measure and tell if you are on track. Here we have a bit of advice: make sure you keep a daily log of your progress with your eating and exercising. Other areas you may want goals include the amount of exercise you do or the number of calories you eat daily. It doesn't matter as long as you are focused on a measurable and time specific goal. Every day note whether you met the goal. If you don't, you need to make it up the next day. This is one of those rare areas you need to monitor very closely. The daily log will solve that problem.

The second area is your personal philosophy/spirituality. The goal in this area can be a bit more complicated. If you attend church, a simple goal like attending weekly is a measurable start. However, there are many other goals you can write for your personal philosophy. You may consider yourself a good family person and therefore you want to structure time for the family to be together every week that can be measured, along with family vacations, etc. The key here is to have thoroughly thought through your philosophy and be able to write it down. When you commit it to paper it becomes real.

Area three is your environment. This includes your clothes, home, car, etc. This is a little easier to write a goal about. During the next year you may have plans to change the carpeting in your house or buy a car. These are easy areas to write down your plans, when you are going to accomplish them, and becomes something you can look forward to.

Next is the area of money. When you think about money, think about dividing your money into four separate pots. Pot one is the amount of money you carry on you. Most people don't carry much because they use credit cards for most transactions. We generally recommend you carry a bit more money. For example, if you carry $20, increase the amount to $110 in various denominations. It will emotionally make you feel wealthier when you look in your wallet and see you have cash available. Overall, it will make you feel more stable. For some, the concept of carrying cash and not spending it can be challenging. There are ads, salesmen, and stores all over trying to influence your spending. It can be a challenge not to spend $7 on coffee just because you have a $10 bill in your pocket. The point of carrying money is to make you feel wealthier and practice self-control in your spending. Stop the impulse spending and see how long you can carry it. At some point, you may end up in a place that only takes cash. You can save the day here! Just do not forget to account for and replace what you've spent.

The second pot of money is your "grab and go money". This is money you keep in a secure place in your home so if there was an emergency you would have, say, $1,000 in cash to handle things until you can get to an area you can use your credit or debit cards. This money, in addition to the cash in your wallet, could come in handy if your bank or credit cards are ever hit by rolling blackouts or other technological issues.

The third pot of money is what you're going to spend in the next 12 to 24 months. This may be money that you are putting in a savings account for a new car, an upcoming vacation, new appliances, and cash for those things you do not want to put on a credit card to avoid paying interest. The nice thing about this pot of money is that it is planned to be spent. This is the money you will spend on gifts and vacations. It helps you in the future so you do not have to take out loans or put balances on high interest credit cards. This is how you can strategically plan to spend your money and prepare for those expenses early.

The fourth pot of money is your wealth fund. This is the money you save toward retirement. This should be invested in stocks, bonds, real estate, or whatever instruments you choose to use and then monitored closely.

The key here is to write goals that will last a year. Each year you want to look at how much money you normally carry in your wallet. Should you increase that by $50 or $100? How much money do you want in your grab and go? Should you change the amount? Will you be purchasing anything new that you need to change the amount of money you will have in your spending account? Finally, how much do you want your wealth account to grow over the next 12-month period? When you think about your goals for money it may be necessary for you to change how you are earning your money. You may need to pick up a second part-time job in order to earn more money to achieve the goals you want. Whatever your goals are, make sure they are realistic and become something you can measure at least a quarterly basis to ensure you are achieving all your goals for the year.

The fifth area is career and work. Your career is vitally important to you and your family. It is critical that you are constantly improving your skill set and becoming more valuable to your company. Only then will you actually be worth more money to the company through promotions and raises that you receive. As you write a goal for your career, consider what education you may need. You may write a goal that says, "I will complete two Microsoft courses in the next year to improve my skills in Word and Excel." These are simple examples. In your career you may have many examples of how you can improve your skill set to become more valuable and make your life more interesting.

The final area is love. This is an area that looks at all of the aspects of love including children, friends, pets, etc. The written goal here may include getting together with friends twice weekly for dinner, a weekly golf outing, or Sunday family dinners. Whatever your goals are, write them down, monitor them, and be sure you complete all of your goals by their deadline.

MOLE Stress

There is a balance of working hard and taking time away to decompress to return mentally stronger. It is an intentional focus on facts, rather than emotions, to reset your focus and gain better control over emotions. MOLEs will often find an activity that helps them be calm. This can include meditation, exercise, therapy, or any other form of emotional control.

To reduce negative stress reactions or symptoms in the future, it is wise to develop organized plans on how to use your time off. This is beneficial because it is planned ahead (not last minute and reactive), gives ample time for you to accomplish your work goals and tasks, and can be a motivator to prioritize properly. Prioritizing your workload allows for an unemotional review as to what is most important at any given time. Learning to properly prioritize and schedule the balance to your work and life will limit stress reactions.

When it comes down to it, humans are flawed and cannot be expected to act perfectly in all situations. Sometimes humans lie or make a mistake and try to cover it up. Tell the truth as much as possible. We're not advising anyone to go out of their way to hurt another's feelings, but even a small lie or avoiding telling the truth can stress the human body. You can see this reflected in lie detector tests. Simply stating your name incorrectly has been shown to result in a physiological stress reaction for many individuals. The best course of action is to try to be honest and when you mess up, remember you are a good person, and do better in the future.

Our minds are amazing things when left alone to dictate our reactions, but sometimes we need to consciously take control and overcome temporary stress. Controlling your emotions will lead you down a more productive and efficient path of making your own life easier. You will be well on your way to becoming a MOLE.

Final Thoughts

It is very important as you write your own strategic plan that you keep these written goals and spreadsheets in a small notebook. As you make daily notes for your health goal, write them on a sheet in the notebook. The notebook will then become your guide to all of your goals over the next year.

Chapter Pearls

- Take care of yourself first (the airline attendant)
- Tend the six gardens of your life
- Develop personal goals and monitor them

| 2 |

Communication and the MOLE

Providing effective communication is one of the biggest problems for any individual and is one of the most identified areas needing improvement by companies. Looking at the problem of improper communication, we see thousands of staff hours and productivity lost trying to clear up miscommunication. We all believe we know how to communicate. You simply talk to someone and they understand what you are telling them. However, that is rarely the way communication occurs.

We will touch on a few of the most prevalent examples of communication in this text, understanding that as technology grows, so will new modes and abilities to communicate. Interpersonal communication means live face-to-face interactions, video conferencing, and phone conversations. Interpretive communication is a receiver's interpretation of the communication to include video message, voicemail, email, text messages, and social media. Presentational communication is one-way communication from a presenter to a group of diverse individuals.

It has been said that only 7 percent of information is transferred from one person to another by words[1]. If you are standing in front of

---
1. Albert Mehrabian and Morton Weiner, "Decoding of Inconsistent Communications," *Journal of Personality and Social Psychology* 6, no. 1 (1967): 109-114.

someone and talking to them, they are picking up 7 percent of their information from the words you use. The other 93 percent comes from the tone you are giving, your body language, and multiple other messages while the two of you are talking.

Humans are prone to hear information and decide if they should believe it and pass it forward. Generally, communication on decisions should go to one up and one down in company hierarchy. So if a person talks with a coworker about a new process or a new plan, both individuals should consider whether a supervisor needs to be told or direct reports need to be told for full and complete communication. Next, they should determine whether other individuals or departments should be aware. This helps eliminate a breakdown in the process later on, acting as a decision tree of sorts. When determining who and when to pass on information, people choose to do so or not for many reasons. This can be due to company culture, feeling like they're tattling on coworkers, or even a feeling like they are not at a level that should report. Organizations need MOLEs who pass all appropriate information forward. Even line level employees can be seen as the canaries in the coal mine. This saying originates from a time when coal miners would bring canaries into the mine with them. If the levels of carbon monoxide reached a point where the canary passed away, then the humans would have enough time to escape before succumbing to the poisonous gas. If front line staff elevate concerns (for example, a nurse who is routinely late and it is bothersome for coworkers) early intervention can be done to help the person adjust their schedule or reset the expectation of their work hours. Without that canary and left for someone else to deal with, the situation can become much larger and could affect client relationships or result in numerous employee losses. Taking all into account, we begin with a discussion on interpersonal communication methods.

Assume Positive Intent

One of the difficulties of effectively communicating is listening to the information without pre-determining the intent. When a coworker brings you information, you internalize what they are saying and the reason they are saying it. Sometimes, an employee will have a negative interaction with a coworker and assume that each time that person comes to them, they want to bring negativity or conflict.

Therefore, a MOLE will allow each interaction to occur separately from prior interactions. Each day is a new opportunity for productivity and collaboration. In one example, we had an employee come up with an idea to track who is on site and who is out of the building. With the growing number of remote workers, the goal was to see how large the office was (even if people were not physically present) and also be aware of who was out on PTO to respect their time (many times remote people get calls on PTO because people do not know they are out of their remote office). When the boards were purchased to be hung, a rumor started that the reason the boards were purchased was so that human resources could see people's coming and going in a negative and micro-managing way. The concept did not make sense, but the rumor passed quickly. There was no positive intent assumed or even a question raised as to why the boards were purchased prior to starting that negative rumor.

In another situation we had an HR employee who would walk the office each morning to say hi to people and again in the evening to ensure she was the last person in the building to lock up. When we moved to a new office in which we did not own the building and did not need to set an alarm, the habit remained as a good way to say hi to people. There was one supervisor who started a rumor in a department that the reason this was occurring was to make sure people were sitting at their desk for every single minute of the day. Again, positive intent was not assumed and unfortunately, the reputation of our HR employee was damaged as a result through no fault of her own. It took months to detect and work through where all this was coming from. By simply choosing to assume positive intent, the question could have been asked of this employee as to why she was walking the office daily. In the end, we know it takes intentional effort to be in a negative and angry state of mind long-term. It causes unnecessary stress on employees and on their peers. A MOLE should consistently analyze the situation and recognize their interpretation of the situation to know if they are assuming positive or negative intent.

It becomes consistently valuable for all of us to think about what we're about to say, and how we're about to say it, prior to opening our mouths and responding. From what we can determine, if you do not naturally assume positive intent of other people in general, you will not perceive yourself as working in a positive work environment and you will likely end that employment. If you feel this negative tendency, it will take additional effort to try to trust others and train yourself to assume positive intent.

Liars

Lying is an intentional action to deceive; it is not to be confused with people who have nervous, knee-jerk responses or make mistakes in conversation. A liar is someone who fails to tell the truth so often that it is assumed by those around them. We have tried for years to not call people liars. We have said they are truth impaired, struggling with the facts, forgetting pertinent information, and perceiving things differently. However, after years of getting creative, we know there are times when we are dealing with liars.

When a MOLE thinks they are dealing with incorrect information from a person, they do not call them a liar. They assume positive intent as a result of an innocent error in communication. First they rule out individuals who are quick to respond. Some individuals have been raised in the workforce that if you do not respond quickly, you are not an expert. They will answer any question you have in an instant and in the way you want it. However, at times, this information is not true or accurate. They panic, they get nervous, and accidentally provide an inaccurate answer. Another version of this is when you tell an employee how you would like them to handle a situation, such as "I'd like you to call this manager and recommend that they do a training log" and the employee responds, "Yes, I've done that" or "I already had that on my list to do." Over time, you will realize as a MOLE that the individual did not truly have that plan or intention but they wanted to please you or for you to think highly of their skills. Give more grace to people in this category than those who are work avoidant or liars.

When dealing with a coworker or employee who is too quick to answer, using very specific questions is a good way to guide them to slow down. If you say, "I would like you to tell the site manager to check the entry logs" and the response is "Yes, I already did," my response back is "You did? When?" Typically they will modify that they mean they already wrote it on their to-do list. Again, you should push, "When did you intend to contact them; who will you call?" As another example, you may ask "Do you know when we scheduled the appointment, was it Tuesday?" and they respond "Yes, I think that's right" without knowing. In that case you may be able to verbalize if they do not know an answer, it is okay if they want to check their notes and get back to you. We do not need immediate answers in most cases and we will be okay with people saying "Let me check my notes" or "I'm not comfortable responding specifically without looking."

Once you rule out that a person is not simply quick to answer and is truly lying, it is time to start documenting. A MOLE always should look at themselves first and this analyzing phase allows you to document specific discussions and interactions to see if they occur the way you agreed they would. This is true whether you are a peer or a supervisor. If you find a peer routinely not telling the truth, it is important to cover your own position and notify the supervisor with facts. An easy way to do this is to start scheduling discussions with the supervisor present or include them in the plans via email.

Most people have good intentions. Liars have a motive. You will come across them from time to time, and in the end, all you can do is start being clear with intentions and documenting when you find them. Over time, your reputation as a MOLE will hold more value than anything a liar could ever say.

Let it Starve

Sometimes it is hard to assume positive intent and not call out a suspected liar. Sometimes an email, text, or similar strikes an emotion within you and you want to respond quickly and directly. When this happens, the reaction is typically done based on emotions and is not well thought out. Commonly if you had let time pass, you would have responded quite differently. Therefore, we have adopted a concept introduced to use by Brittany Krysinski called 'let it starve'. When communication comes to you in a form that causes you to immediately feel an intense emotion, you need to let the message starve. If you receive a text, do not respond to it - let it starve. If you receive an email copying several people that was rude/unproductive/unnecessary, let it starve. Walk away and see if the person reengages in a different form after you've had time to sit with the information. If they say something to your face you can respond, "let me think about that and we can talk later" or "noted" and walk away. Let their comment starve and give them time to think about what they have just communicated. We rarely see an apology out of the original message that we have let starve, however, we regularly see the individual later explain they were having a tough day the prior day or another excuse for the outburst. Additionally, we have had people completely ignore the message and pretend like they never sent it. We love this concept because each time it occurs an unnecessary/unproductive disagreement and conflict has been avoided.

Face-to-Face Communication

The most effective form of communication is face-to-face because you have the best chance of getting the right message across. It allows you to emphasize your words, use body language, eye contact, and all of the interpersonal signals necessary for good communication. Due to the complicated nature of a discussion, you may need to follow up with written documentation of what was agreed upon during your conversation. Even though this is clearly the best way to communicate with people, the truth is both parties must be on the same page for your communication.

Sometime ago we had a problem with the communication of an employee, which resulted in a face-to-face communication going awry. The employee was coming across as a dictator and appeared demeaning to other employees. Her communication style did not work, and it was causing tremendous problems with our clients and staff. We had to remove the employee from a couple of projects. We brought her into the corporate office to spend a few hours working with her and training her to help her understand how she was coming across to people, and to provide suggestions on how to soften her approach. At the end of the training we were satisfied we had helped her understand that she was coming across harshly, which was unacceptable. Weeks went by and the negative behavior continued. Eventually we came to understand that while we had spent time trying to explain how her approach was wrong, she had interpreted the training as trying to help her handle people who were acting dictatorial to her. She completely misunderstood what we were talking about, even though we thought we had been specific.

The personality structure and background she brought to our conversation was such that she could not accept she was not perfect in every way or that she needed to change her behavior and how she handled people. Looking back at this incident, we believe we could have improved our communication with her by being more direct and then following up with written communication to reinforce the points we wanted to make. While we were involved with the training, we should have been looking more deeply into her level of understanding with more questions and engagement to ensure the point was being made and she understood.

Video Communication/Conferencing

The second best form of communication is video communication or video conferencing. There are many different IT systems for video communication that do include less-secure video calls, like Zoom or

FaceTime. Many of them will work as long as you consider the potential privacy issues. You want to be clear you are not violating any state or federal laws, such as HIPAA regulations, by having a communication that may go out to people who have no right to have the information. Once your legal issues are clear, this is a very good form of communication and works quite well. Tele-medicine is growing across the United States and seems to be an example of good communication when you cannot be face-to-face.

Phone Communication

The next best method is the telephone, because the individual can hear not only the words, but also the tone and passion you are bringing to the subject. Since most of us deal with people at a distance, we frequently use the telephone as a form of communication.

Telephone calls should be returned within one to two hours. If you are in a meeting and you are not allowed to bring your phone, you should check your phone periodically throughout the day and upon leaving the meeting. It is important for you to understand that people apply meaning to everything. If they leave a voice message for you and you choose not to get back to them, they may imply you do not think they or their subject are important. They will also be measuring how long it takes you to get back to them.

There was a situation not too long ago where we needed to speak with an employee. We put a call in to her and had no return call within an hour. We then tried a second and third time before giving up. The person returned the call three days later. Our assumption is if she is doing it to us, she is doing it to our clients. Historically, this turns out to be true. Consequently, everyone needs to return missed phone calls in a timely manner.

Video Messages

As we bridge into interpretive communication, a recorded video message is a prime example of the ability to express your information with proper communication strategies, but lacks the ability for the peer-to-peer dialogue to ensure understanding. This means while you may express exactly what you want in tone, behavior, and expression, the message may still be received differently than intended due the lack of interpretation from the individual reviewing it. For example, if you send a video expressing a requirement for a certain dress code at work, but in the video you happened to take your jacket off (which violates that same dress code), then an individual who is watching may interpret the message as 1) not being enforced, or 2) being an unfair rule that does not apply to the sender. Lacking back and forth dialogue can create issues.

Voicemail

Voicemail allows you to express your information with tone and passion, but you are unable to view or hear how the person receives the information. When using voicemail, you must be intentional about what information is being left and not get overly specific. After leaving a voicemail, a MOLE will ensure the message is received by following up in other methods. Assumptions should not be made in case you dialed the wrong number or the message was never heard. We are also becoming aware of individuals who no longer check voicemails. The voicemail-to-text ability for phones is combating this a bit, but on more than one occasion we have heard individuals say, "Don't leave me a voicemail because I won't check it. If I don't answer, text me." As a result of this phenomenon, texting can be combined with voicemail for communication purposes. MOLEs check their voicemail.

Email

Then there is email. As mentioned earlier, only 7 percent of information is transferred from one person to another by words. This means in email you lose 93 percent of communication, which may lead to confusion and misinformation. You cannot control the intended tone of the message or when the message is read. You cannot view how the person receives the information or how they interpreted the message. It is easy to argue that email is among the most common means of communication across the U.S. With that, it's key to understand the basics of sending email properly to your audiences.

Email lives forever. Because of this, we should be careful what we put in an email. Email could someday end up in the hands of a plaintiff's attorney. Consider for a moment all of the chaos that ensued over the emails on politicians' private servers. These emails leaked to multiple other servers, creating great embarrassment and legal risk for the individuals. They thought these emails were so private no one would be able to look at them, but nothing is further from the truth. Everything is recoverable.

As noted earlier, when you are emailing someone, you are dealing with only 7 percent of communication. The odds of it being taken out of context are extremely high. In my opinion, you should not use email for personal issues. Instead you should discuss the issues face-to-face or over the phone. Lengthy emails containing specifics of issues are rarely a good idea. One of the behaviors we have noticed among people who use computers and email a lot is they actually would prefer to sit at their desk and send an email to a coworker 30 feet away, rather than getting up and going to talk to them to ensure the message or information is accurately sent. This aligns with new studies showing that the younger generations would rather send emails than have a face-to-face conversations. This generation makes up a large group of the workforce who were the first to grow up with this technology. This behavior is commonly believed to be due to wanting to reduce small talk, get work done, or do personal things and yet remain in communication sporadically. It is easy to jump in email for short periods of time to continue a chain of messages. The ability to open an email, respond, delete and move on – pushing the task to another person to take action or resolve it on the spot - is largely quick and easy. When you take time to address things face-to-face, you are able to have a meaningful conversation to modify the outcome of the issue. You are also immediately able to discuss other items that may be on either person's mind, resulting in less emailed communication about another topic. There is also a large population of individuals who prefer email due to wanting to think on the subject first. They're not necessarily good at instant responses and would prefer to think before they respond. Email lends to that personality trait nicely. This is possibly also another reason that texting is more common than a phone call.

Email communication can easily go awry. We once had a situation where information was needed in order to meet a sensitive deadline. The person who needed the information emailed the request to another person in the office 30 feet away and included a 5:00 p.m. deadline. The person who sent the email then got busy working on other things and the recipient did not see the email prior to leaving for the day. Both people became angry at each other, but it was all over faulty communication. It is poor practice to email deadline-driven information or requests to someone at your location. Get up, go over, and talk to them. Make sure they understand the importance of what you need, and if needed follow up with a summary email of the verbal conversation.

In another example, two senior executives in different states were emailing back and forth concerning events at a client site. As they continued to email back and forth the tone of the emails began to turn more hostile and it was clear something was wrong in the communication between them. When we finally got involved to try to calm everybody down, it was clear it came down to interpretation of the word "issues." One leader had emailed, "Have you taken care of the issues in Wisconsin?" The leader in Wisconsin interpreted the word issues to mean problems she had generated herself, which was not the intent. She then believed the other leader was becoming accusatory and began to ramp up her emails and became more hostile. This went on for the better part of a day until we got involved, calmed everyone down, and got them on the phone so they could talk to one another. They discovered that in fact their definition of the word "issues" was really the same, it was just what things are you working on, i.e., what issues are you working on? Both leaders were very smart people, but the truth was they liked email far more than talking directly to people, and this caused a considerable amount of trouble.

In most cases email should simply be a way to document verbal conversations in an effort to make sure everybody is on the same page about expectations. Sometime emails appear to be an easy way to transfer information, but more often they delay the solution by hours or days. Picking up the phone would've prevented this issue.

Your company may have a Property and Electronic Communications Systems Policy. You should review the policy and be sure you understand what should and should not be in an email.

Audiences on email can vary. You can send an email to one person, or you can send it to numerous individuals. Just by who you address an email to in the "To" field can determine particular tone or instruction to your message. Let me explain:

If you are choosing to send your email to one person, you should include them solely in the "To" field.

If the message pertains to matters in which your or the recipient's supervisor should be included, place your or their supervisor email address in the carbon copy or "Cc" line. This implies the conversation is intended for the sender and the "To" recipient, but the supervisor can "stay in the loop."

The blind carbon copy, or "Bcc" field allows the "Bcc" recipient to be able to see your initial email to the "To" and "Cc" recipients, while the "To" and "Cc" recipients will not know the "Bcc" recipient is on the email.

For example, if a client reached out to our company president regarding an order, she would direct that request to marketing. The marketing employee would then reach out to the client to confirm a request has been received and has been sent. The employee could put the client email in the "To" line, then put the president on the "Bcc" line to allow the president to see they have responded. The client would not know the president was on the message, but would receive your email message. Even in this scenario, placing the president on the "Cc" line would have been appropriate for the email.

The Problem of Copying Too Many People

When you are determining who needs to have a copy or be aware of an email, always be sure the email is clear about who is responsible for any actions in the correspondence. One of the major problems we have seen is that staff want to be sure they are communicating with everybody and cause tremendous amounts of confusion when they copy too many people and it is unclear who is supposed to do what. We then end up with 8 to 10 people corresponding back and forth to sort out who is to take care of the problem or what their role is in the issue. The bottom line is MOLEs copy who they need to, but don't copy people who are not directly involved.

Drafting Your Message

Composing an email can be quick. Many of us know keyboard shortcuts to open a new message, send a message, delete messages, etc. However, it is key to follow a small checklist when drafting an email each time.

- Enter your recipients appropriately in your addressee fields (To, Cc, Bcc)
- Enter a title in your subject line
- Compose your message
- Include your email signature

Entering Your Subject

A good subject line helps both parties in an email exchange. It should simply provide a brief overview as to what your message will pertain to. For example, if the director of business development is inquiring about a conference in Indianapolis, the subject line could read "Indianapolis, IN Conference".

Composing Your Message Body

You will want to make sure you follow a couple simple guidelines when drafting your messages.

Address the recipient properly: Mr., Mrs., Dr., Ms., etc. for those outside the office/company. If it's between individuals with whom you have a comfortable relationship (using your best judgment), you may address them by their first name. An example would be for a marketing employee to address a vendor representative by their first name after working with them numerous times over the years.

Use complete sentences and proper punctuation. Here is an example of an email that has not used proper sentence structure or punctuation:

"Aja sign up and sponsor the ice cream or the afternoon break send it to Jim Smith at Harvey and Brad Bills a Henry this is a must for the sponsorship send it separate from my registration form do not please send it to the board we have to send it to Jim Smith. thank you so much."

We are not asking you to become a Pulitzer Prize winner, but construct sentences with basic punctuation to help the individuals understand your message. The above message could make the recipient have to read the message three to four times, and even then, not necessarily understand the request. The email should have read:

"Hello John,

There are two remaining opportunities for organizational sponsorship at the upcoming conference taking place on March 12, 2021. One is the Ice Cream Sponsor and the other is the Afternoon Break Sponsor. I recommend you move forward with sponsoring one of these opportunities; both will have similar attendee traffic.

Assuming you choose to move forward, you will need to notify Jim Smith at Harvey County and Brad Bills at Henry County. If you need their emails or phone numbers, I can provide those to you. They will direct you as to where to send the check and the upcoming deadline to commit. Please contact me directly with any questions you may have.

Thank you,

[Signature, including contact information]"

Note: The revised version of the first example used complete sentences, punctuation, and more "please and thank-you's." Additionally, more spaces were added to separate the message. This helps the recipient read the message easier and the paragraphs help separate the phases of the request, such as the registration request in the first paragraph, followed by the sponsorship submission request in the second paragraph.

Your signature should follow at the end of your initial email. Signatures should include your name, title, direct phone number, cell (if necessary), fax, and the website URL. Here is an example:

Joe Smith
Director of Marketing
o: 309.999.1234
c: 309.999.4321
f: 309.999.5432
website URL

Here is a list of strategies MOLEs use to guide them in using email appropriately:

- Keep all messages as brief as possible to minimize reading time for the recipient, thereby keeping communication efficient.
- Be as complete as possible by using the simple rules of who, what, where, when, and why to answer any anticipated questions.
- Avoid communicating through email on a sensitive subject that can be addressed in person.

- Communicate confidential information in another form other than email.
- Check for accuracy and apply all good business writing, using correct grammar, spelling, and punctuation.
- Follow up if a response has not been received in a timely manner.
- Read all messages and respond regularly.
- Avoid typing a message in all capital letters.
- Be careful not to use the "Reply all" function when not necessary or intended, i.e., system-wide distribution.
- Ensure messages are deleted or saved; the server should not be used to permanently store messages.

Texting

The guidelines for texting are similar to those for email communication in that they live forever. Texting should only be used for very specific short messages. You should never discuss personal or sensitive information. In addition, it is not the appropriate method to communicate lengthy discussions or problems or any other issues with staff or clients. An example of an appropriate text would be, "I am leaving work now and will meet with you in about an hour" or "I need to change the time of our video conference with our new employee, call me to reschedule." These are very brief examples of appropriate texts.

Remember that email and texts are not private. Think of the problems politicians had during the 2016 election. 2016 marked the first time politicians used the text messaging feature to encourage voters to show support and make campaign donations. It also was the first time the ability to contact voters via phone was reviewed from the legal standpoint of whether the person opted in to receive presidential solicitation. This practice sparked some individuals to send fake campaigns via text messaging such as "text in your vote," which is not an acceptable method of voting. Be very careful with the information you send via a text message and ensure you know who is on the other end of the phone. Failing to act cautiously with confidential medical or personal information can result in future lawsuits for all parties involved, even if you are put on the group message. Any text message may be screen captured, printed, emailed, and sent for someone else's own personal gain. Do not put anything in a message that may be embarrassing.

Social Media

Much further down the line are newer forms of communication including social media. Social media comes into play when we are trying to communicate with large numbers of individuals. Social media includes Facebook, Instagram, TikTok, LinkedIn, and blogs, and allow for communication with a lot of people instantly. Whatever is posted is up to individual interpretation. Furthermore, social media has the ability to quickly spread false information even if it was not the original intent of the poster. Comments, sarcasm, and jokes can be deemed appropriate or not appropriate by large masses of individuals and are unable to be permanently taken back or deleted. People's lives have been forever changed as a result of online social media posting. Be aware of what you put out into the world.

Providing thoughts and opinions on social media solicits feedback, and not always in a supportive way. When you couple emotional statements with false assumptions and no data, it opens you up to critical review and can become a conflict of interest in a role. MOLEs work to process their emotions in productive ways, rather than post outbursts in a social forum. This is not to say that MOLEs avoid standing up for what they believe in or refuse to take a stand on what they believe is right, but MOLEs post information with clear intention. A MOLE, for example, would not post about their terrible supervisor, because the social environment has no control over their supervisor's employment or behavior. Instead, a MOLE would notify human resources or another member of management. MOLEs do not cyberbully or make false assumptions about what a company or person cares about or does not care about. MOLEs know the difference between personal opinions/beliefs and false or emotional statements relating to a specific person/event/scenario.

Learning Management Systems and Large Meetings

As a MOLE employee you will experience presentational communication when utilizing a learning management system for training and when going to meetings and conferences. While they may be in a live or pre-recorded video format, the communication style largely is one sided without the back and forth dialogue of true face-to-face communication. Feedback opportunities are limited and information is given either through spoken words, written words, or with visual presentations. While it is a good way to get training and memos out to a large population of people, much of the supporting communication factors are absent.

Transactional Analysis Theory

In the book *I'm OK—You're OK*, written by Thomas A. Harris, there is a breakdown of the ego states in which people operate and communicate: the parent, the adult, the child. We have found this concept useful when working with employees on how to speak with one another, no matter what mode of communication they find to be most appropriate for the situation. Professional communication is speaking on an adult adult level at work whenever possible.

The Parent

As a small child, you will remember the parent was a big person that spoke with authority. Generally there was no area for discussion, and at times, parents could be quite dictatorial. There was a good purpose for this when you were a small child and did not yet have the experience to do things in a way that would keep you safe. The parent may say, "Do not play in the street," "Do not touch that burner," or "Always look both ways before you cross the street." For the child these are good parental rules to follow. However, for adult communication being a parent or dictator does not work.

The Child

The second state is the child. The child is emotional and can feel the results of the communication very strongly. When communicating the child will frequently cry or be apologetic. The overall communication style is emotional and not necessarily logical. For adults, communicating as a child will not work.

The Adult

As we mature to an adult, we can combine the ability to recall the lessons learned from the parent and experiences of the child. Now, we have the ability to put them in their proper place. An adult stays calm and does not act as a parent or be demanding during communication. The adult is reasonable, logical, and calmly makes their point. It is important to try to stay in the adult at all times during your communication.

Suppose an employee speaks from the perspective of a parent and says, "You're using this form all wrong and you should know better." The person they are talking to must decide about how to respond. For example, they can respond from their parent, "No I am not, and you should know better than that." They could respond from their inner child, "I'm so sorry I didn't know, I'll never do it again, I'm the worst." The proper way to respond is to step back, analyze the situation, and decide if they have really made a mistake. If so, respond, "I see what you mean, and I will do it differently next time." It is important to understand that when you are talking to somebody, using the *I'm OK—You're OK* format, you always need to stay in your perspective as an adult. That is sometimes difficult if someone is raising their voice and speaking from their perspective as a parent, but if you continue to speak from your perspective as an adult they will eventually have to stop yelling and move on.

The main thing to understand about the communication is if lines remain parallel from parent to child and child back to parent or from adult to adult, the discussion can go on virtually forever. If you are to break the conversation you must try to cross lines or move parallel lines apart. For example, if someone talks to your child you should move to the adult and speak back to their adult, which will generally stop the whiny conversation. In the example above where a team member is saying, "You are using this form all wrong and you should know better," he is speaking from his parent down to your child. If you speak from your adult to his adult it will cross lines and will stop the angry conversation. Always remember as long as you stay in the adult you will stay in control of these conversations.

As you look closely at the three circles with the parent, adult, and child, watch your cohorts and listen to how they are talking. What mode are they currently in? Are they complaining bitterly about something and are somewhat loud in the parent? Are they talking logically and acting as an adult, or are they whining or complaining about something as a child—"Ain't it awful, nobody cares around here." What mode are they in at any given time? As you practice watching other people talk, you will tend to get stronger and stay in your own adult for your own communication.

The 12 Step Approach to Dealing with People

The 12 steps listed below were originally designed to defuse potentially confrontational situations and help you navigate difficult discussions with a minimum of trouble. It turns out the same 12 step approach can be used with anyone with whom you have to deal. Examples include a client, your supervisor, or even an employee.

Step 1. Do not be confrontational.

Recognize you both have different backgrounds, experiences, and perceptions of the same situation. Some people tend to deal with potential conflict by starting off defensive and direct. If this is a tendency of yours, start the discussion by asking more questions, rather than telling the person what you believe to be true. Failing to start the discussion calm may place the other individual at a heightened state of agitation and defense as well leading to confrontation. Even if the other person is being confrontational, you should be quiet, stay calm, and utilize the tips and techniques shared later in this book. Being confrontational will simply accelerate the situation and make things worse. Confrontation may come in the form of elevated voices, exaggerated movements, verbal personal attacks, and/or physical advances. As voices are raised, people stop listening. Remember, just because someone is the loudest person in the room does not mean they are correct. If you do not match the confrontation level, it will be very difficult for them to continue at the heightened level of performance very long.

Step 2. Listen without interrupting.

The person with whom you are dealing has an issue and they want to make sure you understand. Do not interrupt—let the person get everything out. If you choose to challenge and respond to each point a person is making, chances are they will continue to explain their points and elevate the discussion. Waiting until the end allows the person to tell you every single concern, issue, and/or grievance they have. Sit back, give them time, and listen. You will have a full picture of exactly what you should respond to. If you start to respond and they begin to respond again, sit quietly and let them get it all out again. Then start over.

Step 3. Use a sad, but glad statement.

Express empathy, acknowledge concern, and share a solution. It generally goes something like this: "While I certainly understand why you would feel that way given the situation, the good news is we can solve this problem very easily." This is a sad but glad statement.

In a workplace situation, this interaction may go something like this:

Employee: "What is wrong with people today! Everyone I talk to is mad about something and there are fires everywhere!"

Supervisor: "Gosh, it sounds like today is becoming pretty challenging! But the good news is I'm here to help. What do you need from me - to just listen to what is going on, help coming up with a plan to deal with priorities today, or assistance in doing a task or two?"

This acknowledges the whirlwind of the day and offers a few different solutions for the individual to choose from, giving them control of the solution. By offering options, the individual can decide if they want help or if they just needed to verbalize the concern out loud. You're requesting clear expectations and can get a plan they're on board with.

Step 4. Express empathy.

Most people in the world want to avoid conflict and want the best outcome for everyone involved. Therefore, it is hard to stay angry at a person who expresses genuine concern and is listening. Put simply, people have difficulty being angry with people who are empathetic. Voicing the understanding in your sad but glad statement expresses empathy, but that's not where it stops. You are choosing to put your differences aside and connect with them on a human level of understanding. Again, that does not mean the other person's view or point is accurate or valuable. It means you want them to feel settled and resolve the situation for the positive.

In one of our leadership training examples, we use the story of Nurse Aww. Nurse Aww represents a clear example of the type of empathy we promote. For example, let's say you are a nurse working in a correctional environment. A patient who is brought to you has started several fights and requires extra security, for your safety, while you address the medical sick call. When the patient presents with a hangnail which is causing discomfort, what would your reaction be? In the case of Nurse Aww, the patient is greeted with the response, "Aww, I understand this is causing you discomfort." The simple "aww" statement expresses empathy and understanding. This allows the patient to know you care about what they are saying and are listening to their complaint/needs. Should the patient be met with sharp, judgmental comments such as "this is not a big deal" or "why are you coming to me with this", a barrier will be put between the two individuals causing anger and frustration. One of our most tenured nurses uses this strategy and, to date, has not been sued by a patient.

In the workplace, this could translate to an employee being fearful of catching an illness in the office. Telling the employee to "suck it up" or asking them if they want their job creates barriers immediately. Instead, try channeling your inner Nurse Aww and respond, "Aww, I understand you feel concerned/worried, let's discuss what options we have at this point and how you would like to move forward." In this situation, it opens the door to allow discussions for remote work, paid time off, and/or other flexible options- even if the result is the employee should come to work if they want to be paid and continue employment. The empathetic response starts the conversation on a collaborative discussion field. That being said, you will need to adopt your own version of the empathetic response as "aww" may not be appropriate for you and your personality. Additionally, we're not suggesting that the entire population suddenly begin using "aww" in everyday language and interactions. What we promote is an immediate emotional understanding verbalized in a way that is to be universally perceived as fair and accepting. Your technique may be intentionally putting down your phone and closing your computer screen when someone brings up a difficult topic or maybe your verbalized response is a sentence such as "I hear what you're saying; how can I help?"

When discussing this subject, Dr. Johnson is often reminded of a show on television years ago called New Amsterdam. In the series the main doctor operated under the empathetic Nurse Aww statement of "how can I help?" While he rarely was popular with people initially due to his personality tendencies, the statement let coworkers know he was there to listen, learn and work collaboratively. Expressing empathy through adopting your own Nurse Aww statement will assist you in being a MOLE leader.

Step 5. Ask questions to clarify the issues.

This will help you ensure you do understand. Asking questions allows you to hear exactly what the pain points are in the situation. It allows you to hear what you need to respond to and find out if it is something you can resolve. What is the real reason that you are having this discussion? Is it the obvious issue at hand, or is it a continuance of annoyances over a period of time? Look below the surface with your questions and learn all you can.

Step 6. Find out what the person wants.

If you do not know what the person wants or what the goal of the conversation is, it is necessary to ask. Do not be afraid to ask what the point of the meeting or discussion is. The more open, straightforward communication can happen, the less potential for misinterpretation. If you are unsure of what to ask, just ask them, "In your opinion, how would you like to see this resolved?" In many cases, they will tell you their ideal outcome.

Step 7. Repeat back to the person exactly what they said so you are both certain you understand the problem.

Repeating back what you heard is an excellent way to ensure you received the information the way they intended to send it. Two people can walk out of a room with very different perceptions of a conversation. Make sure you have repeated the problem back clear enough so you both agree on the issue you are discussing. It will save you confusion later on.

Step 8. Explain what you can and cannot do given the situation.

Many times, this can be done though saying, "What I am hearing is [explain what they told you] and your ideal outcome is [explain what they told you]. What I can do right now is [give a solution, i.e., make a call to a resource]. What I will be unable to do is [tell them the specific thing you cannot do]. I cannot do this because [give the reasons, i.e., my medical licenses will not allow me to]. I understand why this can be frustrating because I understand your concern. Should I move forward?" In the end, you are asking their acceptance of the plan of action of what you can do. You are telling them exactly what you can do and they are given the choice to allow you to help. It will be unlikely they refuse your help.

Step 9. Discuss possible alternatives to what they want and see if they are acceptable.

Talk through all possible alternatives using the sad but glad responses to include what you can and cannot do. Do this for each alternative provided. When appropriate, direct the individual back to what you can do to steer the conversation back on track. Shutting down their ideas too quickly may be perceived as a personal attack on them, and the confrontation level may start to rise again.

Step 10. Take appropriate action.

When you have come up with a solution or something you can do, take action. Do not let this fall off. Follow through is one of the most important pieces of effective communication because it can build or destroy trust.

Step 11. Follow up to ensure the action has been completed and things are going well.

Following up builds trust and ensures that once an issue has been resolved, you do not forget about it. This shows you care about the other individual involved and are focusing on ensuring the same issues do not happen again after you take the time to resolve it. You should not operate under an "out of sight out of mind" mindset. An example of this would be during a meeting, an issue comes up and a client becomes agitated about lack of performance of someone else in your company. The employee dutifully notes this in the action items and then follows up with the person who did not perform adequately to ensure that everything is resolved and taken care of to the client's satisfaction. One method of follow up you may use is the 2/4/6 method outlined later in this book.

Step 12. Maintain relationships.

It can be tempting to avoid individuals who you find consistently difficult to work with, however, maintaining a relationship builds stronger lines of communication and trust. Not only may they not wait as long to notify you when they have a concern, but if issues do arise in the future, they may react in less of a heightened or agitated way toward you.

The 12 step approach should be used whenever you're dealing with an individual who has a concern or problem. Once you become proficient in these 12 steps, you will be able to handle virtually any situation that arises. As you are going through the steps always stay in the ego-state of the adult. The trick in this system is to not be confrontational, stay in the adult, use the sad but glad statement, express empathy, and follow up.

Pass Information, Not Fear

No matter what form of communication you ultimately choose to transfer the message through, do a quick review of your goal/point of the conversation. You will need to ensure you are passing the facts of the situation and not the fear, or emotional component. For example, we had a situation where a client was upset that a nurse stopped showing up for work. No one had notified the supervisor and now the client was so upset that they demanded a member of the executive team attend.

The executive team member was told by the supervisor that the client would be very angry when they came to visit and to be prepared to be screamed at. This made the executive team member nervous, so they requested a coaching session with Dr. Moriarity to prepare to meet with the client. What she uncovered in the conversation was that the details of the actual issue were not mentioned when this executive was told to go to see the client. The supervisor did, however, tell the executive to be prepared to be yelled at, placing them in a defensive mindset (over someone they did not know and who was not showing up for work). No one would be excited about that type of situation. Once Dr. Moriarity realized this, they further consulted with the supervisor for details.

In the end, they agreed that at the client meeting, their position was on the same team as the client. They, too, were not pleased the nurse failed to show up to work. They decided to use this as an opportunity to notify the client that they agreed and understood their frustration, and they also disagreed with the way the nurse handled the situation. Dr. Moriarity and the executive then developed solutions to provide the client so it would not happen again. When the executive team member met with the client, the executive team member was no longer defensive and nervous. They knew and understood the facts, and they matched the client's issues! The meeting went well, and it became an internal reminder and lesson to pass the information, not the fear to coworkers.

Viral Conversations

Incorrect thoughts can infect a person or group of people like a virus. In the book *Games People Play* by Eric Berne, he talks about a game called "Ain't it Awful?" This is used to strike up a conversation with a stranger by getting them to agree with some negative concept or viral thought.

It goes like this: two women are sitting at a bus stop and they don't know each other. One says to the other, "Ain't it awful? This bus is never on time." The woman simply expressed a thought and her opinion. The second woman must make a decision on how to respond. As noted in *I'm OK—You're OK*, the first person made her statement as a child. This is a whiney, complaining statement frequently witnessed in children. The other woman now has a choice to respond as an adult, "I really haven't noticed that, I think it's on time." The conversation will probably stop. If she wants to keep the conversation going, she can respond in her child by saying something like, "Ain't it awful? You're right, I can't remember the last time this bus was on time." This will continue the conversation.

They can keep that conversation going easily, while others around them are hearing the conversation. Even if one person thinks the bus runs efficiently, the conversation they are overhearing may change their mind and now they are thinking to themselves, "You know, I thought the buses ran on time, but they may be right."

All of a sudden, because of this one negative statement, they have infected other people around them with that thought. Now you have 100 people down at city hall asking for the director of transportation to explain why the busses are always late, when in fact they are running on time.

Viral Thoughts

Viral thoughts can start frequently in a company. We have witnessed many examples of this. As a MOLE, it will be your job to look for viral thinking in your team members and stop it by discussing the problem from your adult. Give them facts and prevent incorrect viral thinking from taking over.

Viral thoughts commonly occur when a company grows large enough to support remote workers. Team members get to know one another through word of mouth and perceptions are formed. Whatever is unknown can be easily filled in by making assumptions lacking any fact to prove or disprove the comments.

Let's assume an organization has a single corporate office with managers who travel to various locations. The manager, Sarah, is traveling to a location and she is undergoing performance issues for not showing up to meetings on time. Sarah is late to the office and has recently started showing up late to client meetings. Commonly, employees such as Sarah who are undergoing issues do not fully admit to their own wrongdoing when expressing frustration. Instead to release frustration, Sarah vents to a coworker named Mark, who does not have a personal relationship with Sarah's supervisor to refute the information that Sarah is 1) being micromanaged, 2) that Sarah's good work is not being appreciated, and 3) that Sarah has a lot of family things going on that no one cares about.

Pieces of this viral talk are true:

1. Sarah's manager may be micromanaging Sarah as a result of the performance issues and as a result of clients and coworkers complaining. Sarah's time may be temporarily focused on by her supervisor until it is corrected. However, chances are if this was a historical micromanaging event, Sarah would not have been able to be late this many times without earlier discussions.
2. Sarah stating that her good work is not being appreciated is an attempt for her to defend being late. "All of the work" that Sarah does after arriving is not being challenged and is not relevant. Sarah's manager simply wants Sarah to show up when she committed to. Furthermore, most meetings with staff and clients are set up by employees together. Any meetings Sarah has been late to have been set up by Sarah herself. She should not be late regularly since she controls her own schedule.
3. Finally, commenting about personal issues results in remote/distant staff, such as Mark, believing that Sarah's manger, of whom he does not know, does not care about personal lives, which is a fabrication lacking any details or proof. If employees are sick, if a car breaks down, if events occur, it is in the company's best interest to work with an employee. But when the issues are ongoing and become a regular habit to the point there are attendance concerns, the issues become less of a personal attack against Sarah's personal life and instead her manager's role in ensuring the work Sarah was hired to do gets completed. It is

not fair to other employees when a handful of people, such as Sarah, are able to come and go as they please without being held to the attendance expectations. It is also unfair to the employee that their reputation is being damaged.

When this occurs, it is usually done under the radar and fear is created in the field. Any communication or interaction that Mark now has with Sarah's manager will be under a jaded lens. If Sarah's manager is talking to Mark about a site issue, it may seem to prove Sarah's information correct. Mark must understand that there is some truth in venting, but also that he does not have all of the information to make a personal judgment.

Negative thoughts can spread. No one wants to be in a negative environment. We have all sat next to the person at work or at a restaurant that did not have anything positive to say.

It's important to understand that in every viral conversation there may be a grain of truth. For example, if two team members are talking negatively in a viral manner about a third employee, it may be that they have a point, but their method of handling it is inappropriate. MOLEs master the ability to hear viral conversations and sort through to find the potential issue. They then, without spreading the gossip, investigate the potential issue. For example, if two employees are in the kitchen gossiping that the company is "so cheap" they do not even provide pens for employees, you can imagine how quickly the news may spread. This would extend to employees noticing other areas the company could have cut corners. Directions from management may now be perceived as negative and lacking support or assistance. A MOLE would hear that information and go ask the person in charge of supplies why no pens were ordered. There would be a response, most likely, that indicates no one put in a request to replenish the storage room with pens and they didn't realize it was a current issue. Pens would then be ordered. Another response may be that the specific pens were not reordered for a reason such as the supplier being out of stock or similar.

The point is, a MOLE does not simply agree with negativity, they get a reason. MOLD fuels negativity and gossip until everyone becomes zombies.

Zombies

There is a story about a colony of ants in the Amazon. An ant colony is a perfect communication network. Each ant knows their respective job and they execute those jobs immediately. If there is an attack on the ant colony, those ants that take care of the queen will move her to a safer location. Those that are taking care of the eggs will begin to move them to a better spot. The construction ants will wall up certain tunnels and start to build other tunnels. The army ants will head out to fight off whatever is attacking the colony.

Sometimes there is a parasite or a virus in the soil that will infect one of the ants. When this happens, it changes the ants' behavior and they walk around aimlessly. With the colony under attack, all of the ants are busily running around doing their job except for the one ant who is wandering around like a zombie. Once the colony is safe again and the attack has been stopped, the healthy ants gather around the one that is wandering around and not doing their job, and quickly kill it. It's pretty clear we cannot do that for zombie employees, but zombie employees are real, and their apathy is a problem.

Zombie employees are just going through the motions. They don't care about what they are doing, don't care what the results are, and are just putting in the time because they have the viral thought that management does not care. Viral conversations cause zombies in the following ways:

One employee says to another, "Ain't it awful they just don't care around here? They don't care about us or what we do." This clearly is an incorrect thought, but there may be other people who begin to agree without asking questions. Before long, there are a number of people that are not putting in any effort. They do not think anybody cares. They do not see any reason they should be productive, because nobody cares.

Zombie employees are unproductive and can be dangerous to other employees. If you believe you have a zombie employee, you will need to address this with them and come up with a plan to correct the behavior, or that employee will be lost.

Vampires

Vampires suck energy and time from you. Vampires are employees who are passionate about how they are perceived by other employees. For example, an employee may get the idea that another individual in the company believes they are not doing their fair share of work or have been verbally demeaning to them in some way. The employee then contacts their supervisor to explain why this is not true and how they would not do such a thing. Even after they have explained themselves to their supervisor, the employee simply will not let it go. They may call back multiple times to discuss the same issue. The telephone calls will end up eating your time and energy as you keep trying to reassure the employee that you understand what they are talking about and that they are okay, because there is no issue to resolve.

It has been Dr. Johnson's observation that vampires come from deep-seated concerns of inadequacy. Consequently, they are difficult to deal with. The method you should use requires identifying their form of communication as inappropriate, excessive, and energy draining. We recommend writing it down for your quarterly coaching sessions, so you have the ability to bring it up every three months to discuss how they are doing with it. In the meantime, when the employee calls back again with an energy draining conversation, you can cut it shorter and point out this is what you were talking about in their quarterly review. Using this technique over a period of time actually does reduce the problem and makes the employee more comfortable. Remember that one of the reasons employees do this is that they are not sure about you and your opinion of them. You can only reassure them so much, and at that point, you are done, and it is time to move on. You have every right to say that. You do need to write it down so that you can bring it up again later to measure and ensure this is not happening.

There is more time and productivity lost through poor communication than anything else. Strive to be well understood and to understand. If you are not clear at the end of the conversation, ask specific questions, repeat the expectations back, or call the person back. You should be clear in your mind before you move forward.

Chapter Pearls

- Choose the proper method to communicate
- Send messages (emails, texts, social media, etc.) like you're announcing it to a plaintiff's attorney
- Speak to individuals at the proper level (parent, adult, child)
- Use the 12 step approach for dealing with people
- Pass information, not fear
- Avoid viral conversations
- Identify zombies and vampires

| 3 |

Execution and the MOLE

The definition of execution is the carrying out or putting into effect a plan, order, or course of action. The ability to execute is the single most important value a MOLE can possess. Without execution, plans are not completed, projects are not done, and companies do not survive. Execution is paramount.

As employees are hired into any company, they come with various levels of ability to execute. It is our firm belief everybody can improve their level of execution if the company has laid out a consistent structure of communication that supports, monitors, and enforces execution. You can have an employee who has the best strategic plan, the best training, and the best goals, but if they cannot execute none of that matters. MOLEs by their very nature are exceptionally good at execution and generally have developed techniques to help them execute and complete their daily work. It has been our experience that there are techniques you can teach that will help anyone execute at a higher level. When one couples the techniques with monitoring to ensure they are executing, the results can be amazing.

11:00 Rule

Normally you come to work with an idea of what you would like to get accomplished, and as you organize your work for the day and get started the phone rings and you are immediately taken in another direction. You handle the problem in 10 to 15 minutes and start back on the project you would like to complete, and then an employee comes in to talk about a budget on which they need help. Once again you have to stop what you are doing to work with that employee. At times two or three people might be standing outside of the office door, waiting to come in one after another. This prevents staff from getting any projects done on which they wanted to work. These are examples of the whirlwind as discussed in the book *The 4 Disciplines of Execution* by Chris McChesney, Sean Covey, and Jim Huling.

The whirlwind is ongoing and constant. If you do not try to take control of it, it will control you. The trick here is to slowly train people about what time of the day you would like to reserve for yourself and what times of the day would be best for collaboration with other people. Generally, it takes a long time to train everybody, particularly those who work remotely. If you continue to work on it, you will eventually reduce the amount of whirlwind calls you get during those times you prefer to focus on your main objectives.

While we agree all of the people lined up outside of the office door needed to talk, it was not clear they needed to talk at exactly that moment. For example, if they had just completed a budget and wanted to talk about the details, did it have to be done at 9:30 in the morning or could it wait until after 11:00 in the morning? The answer was almost always that it could be discussed later. Once we began to look at this concept of no interruptions before 11:00, it was clear that productivity would improve if no one interfered with other employees before 11:00. They all could come to work and be reassured that from 8:00 to 11:00 a.m. no one would bother them as long as they didn't bother anyone else. If they completed work that needed the opinion of another employee, they would set it aside and start to work on the next project until 11:00 a.m., then they could start moving around and working with other employees. At that point, we wrote the 11:00 a.m. rule and established it throughout the company.

Try to focus on your work until 11:00 a.m., try not to call other employees unless it is an emergency. Try not to walk into other people's offices before 11:00 in the morning, because they need to get their work done, too. We went so far as to make up signs that said "11:00 Rule" and put them on the outside of the doors with the door shut if possible. Those working in cubicles without doors simply hung a sign. MOLEs can train their direct reports to try to hold their questions until after 11:00 and try to practice it themselves. Productivity and execution will improve.

When implementing the 11:00 Rule in your own organization or department, be mindful of employee start times. Typically, our office is open at 8:00 a.m., therefore 11:00 a.m. is three hours after the start of most shifts. In your organization, this time may be later or earlier in the morning to accomplish your goals.

Meetings

When a topic needs to be discussed on a regular basis, a reoccurring meeting should be set. Minutes should be taken in a standardized format. The format of the minutes should include the date and time of the meeting, attendees, and an agenda. Meetings should aim to last no more than an hour if at all possible. The purpose of the meeting should be at the top of the agenda to have as much focus and attention to it as possible. Typically, the main point will focus on advancing the particularly important goal (PIG) in the organization by communication and decision-making.

During the meeting a standardized approach should be taken to document what occurred or what was approved. Each individual has a place in the meeting to report their status or progress in helping to meet the goals. The person taking minutes should create "action items" in order to encourage movement by the next meeting and assign meeting participants to complete it.

Meetings are typically about reporting but could be a brainstorming session. Attendees should be focused on the overall vision and mission of the meeting. Attendees should be constantly asking themselves how they can help advance the goals of others or pave the way by breaking down barriers that slow progress. They should not zone out in areas they are not reporting in and become meeting tourists.

Meeting Tourists

Meeting Tourists are individuals who do not prepare for a meeting but come because they believe they must. They do not intend to speak up and participate; instead, they are there for entertainment. They may present as distracted, checking their phone, or bored in meetings.

Everyone attending must have a responsibility to the meeting, such as to report on something or to be directly involved in an issue discussion. MOLEs come prepared. All organizations hold regular meetings to collaborate and provide status updates. A MOLE is not a meeting tourist. Review the meetings you attend at your organization to ensure you are productive and efficient. If you are not actively participating in a meeting, determine if you need to be in the meeting at all.

Commitments

With the cadence of meetings varying from weekly to monthly, it is important employees think about the most important things they can do in the next seven days to help the company accomplish their particularly important goal (PIG). These are called commitments. Commitments cannot be broken, and they must be properly written.

An example of a proper commitment is, "I will complete the contract with company XYZ by next week." When the weekly meeting occurs the employee then reports they completed the contract and the results of their commitment. What happened to the contract, where did it go, was it accepted, etc.

A poorly written commitment would be, "I will talk to Mr. Jones on Tuesday concerning expanding services." On Tuesday, the employee calls Mr. Jones and finds out he is on vacation for the next ten days. Therefore, the employee is unable to complete this commitment. The reason it was a poorly written commitment is because he relied on someone else (Mr. Jones) as opposed to relying on his own work. Always consider this when writing commitments. All commitments must be completed.

Action Items

For every meeting action items, changes, or improvements in the company, must be developed. If there are no action items, there was no purpose of the meeting. Consequently, it is not uncommon that as you attend a number of meetings throughout the week you will begin to pick up a few action items that need to be completed by a particular timeframe. These action items from all the various committee meetings are then transferred to the Monday staff meeting and reviewed weekly to ensure they are completed and executed in a timely manner.

Properly done, action items can be a very powerful way to not only help with execution but to measure execution. You can look at the due dates and figure out the percent of time you executed within an allotted time. If you had an action item due a week ago, did it get done or did it take longer? The two main reasons action items are not completed in a timely manner are poorly written action items with unrealistic expectations or you simply forgot about it. Keeping the action items in front of you at all times will help you execute.

Notebooks and Records

It has been our experience that people who carry notebooks into every meeting and interaction with other employees and write things down tend to be the people that execute and get things done. It doesn't matter if it's a hand-written notebook or an electronic device. Keeping all of your notes in one place also cuts down on the likelihood that you'll lose notes written on a single piece of paper. Review your records and notes first thing in the morning, periodically throughout the day, and at the end of the day to ensure you are executing at the level you expect of yourself.

2/4/6 Programs

One of the best ways to monitor programs is called the 2/4/6 program because "stuff happens." When we have a problem with a distant client, we frequently will send one to three people in to resolve the problem. This may take one or two days. At the end of that time the issue is resolved, everything is back to normal and functioning well. It is not uncommon, however, if we leave the site and do not follow up adequately in one to two months, the problem will return as if we were never there in the first place.

Based upon this problem we developed a 2/4/6 program, which states that after you leave the site where you have to correct a problem, in two days you will call back and specifically see how the solution to the problem is progressing. Have people started to fall back into their same behaviors? Have they made the changes you recommended? Are they handling it correctly? You will call again on the fourth day and again on the sixth. At the end of the conversation on the sixth day it will become clear to your staff at the distant site you are going to keep calling and you are going to stay on this. They know they are being monitored and they are going to have to watch what they are doing and stay on top of it. The likelihood this is going to be completed and people aren't going to fall back into their prior behavior is now very high. At the end of the third phone call you let them know you'll be calling back at some point. They will probably assume it is going to be two days, but truthfully you may be able to wait a week or 10 days before you call the next time. Continue to follow up and ensure it's never going to happen again. This 2/4/6 program is one of the most powerful monitoring systems we have been able to develop. When employees have to develop a 2/4/6 program, we expect them to write down brief details and report them in their quarterly coaching meetings.

Every fall we meet for about a week with all the senior leadership in the company to determine any changes in our marketing and our new strategic plan going forward for the next year. The main goal of the company is financial, and it is the particularly important goal (PIG). Out of the meeting comes many action items which are assigned to specific people with specific time frames for completion. All those action items are transferred to our weekly staff meetings to be monitored for completion. This ensures execution of all those action items. If problems arise and certain action items cannot be completed, we have the strength of the leadership to try to clear the way and assist in getting them done and executed on time.

When the company strategic plan is done it includes an evaluation and rewriting of the purpose, vision, and mission statements. Each division then reviews their mission statements and rewrites them as necessary to ensure they are accomplishing the things that need to be executed over the next year. From that, new goals are written for the department and new action items from each division are determined, which once again are brought to the weekly staff meeting so we can monitor execution and completion.

The weekly meeting then becomes the central clearinghouse of all action items and acts as a communication hub and monitoring center to ensure each department and leaders are executing on a regular basis. Records are kept of the number of action items and completion dates. These are reported during coaching sessions, so we can document execution as part of the overall employee evaluation.

There are many subcommittee meetings that take place in addition to division meetings and the weekly staff meeting. These may include finance, training, recognition, and many others. Each meeting must have action items, or the meeting was a waste of time. Once the meeting is concluded, the action items are documented and sent to the regular weekly meeting. This forces each individual to report on an execution status weekly so it does not fall off their to-do list. In the end, a system of meetings, action items, and monitoring becomes the framework to guarantee execution.

This is not difficult in the corporate office. It becomes more difficult when you consider we have employees in hundreds of projects throughout the United States. These individuals have job descriptions which must be executed, and it is not unusual that their superiors will only visit their sites six or seven times a year. Because of this, it becomes critical that execution reviews are performed at each visit to ensure that the work is getting done and things are being properly handled. For this we use checkoff sheets, telephone contact, email, and a system of routing quality assurance meetings at each site to guarantee execution and completion of all duties. In the end it is critical for all leaders to set up a structure of monitoring and execution that will allow their department or company to achieve all its goals. In addition to the annual strategic plan meeting, senior leadership meets every three months to reevaluate exactly where we are on metrics and any changes in the marketplace. This allows us to make course corrections and to stay on track. Then, lengthy peer reviews/coaching sessions with each senior leader occur every three months. These reviews go into detail over their goals, how they are handling their action items, and any other items, which may be affecting their performance.

Execution Score

As you attend meetings to report on your commitments and gather action items, it is equally important you follow through on completing what you say you will do. This is called execution. This is a skillset that does not come naturally to people because of competing priorities. The goal is, whenever you say you will complete something by a specific date, you need to follow through and do it. From time to time a commitment or an action item has to be delayed and it is okay as long as it is not a habit. For example, if you are committed to calling a client by the end of the week and your excuse is the week got away from you, you failed at that commitment. You had told everyone that was the single most important thing you could do that week, and you did not do it. However, if you told everyone you were committed to meeting face-to-face with a client by the end of the week and then you are told not to come due to a pandemic outbreak, then it is reasonable to adjust the commitment for completion.

An execution score should be calculated on your ability to meet your chosen deadlines. There are no extra points for doing something early, but you are penalized for completing it late. Therefore, if you have an action item to complete a task by Friday and you complete it on Wednesday, you met your action item. If you complete the task on Friday, you also completed that action item. If you did not complete the task until Saturday, now you have failed to meet one action item. How many items you did or did not complete can have a substantial effect on your execution percentage. If you have two action items this week and only one completed on time, you're at a 50 percent. Twenty action items and 19 complete, you're at 95 percent.

Failing to execute and follow through on the things you say you will do will get noticed by your peers, and your ability to build strong, productive, and dependable relationships with one another can be damaged. MOLE employees follow through and communicate if there are any bumps along the way. Do not put the burden on someone else to tell you if you are failing to meet your action items and do not blame others if you fail to complete them. By choosing the action item and assigning the deadline, they are your responsibility to complete.

Final Tips

Execution is where the rubber meets the road. People who don't execute will not be MOLEs. They will not make your life easier, and you will constantly have to prop them up and get them refocused on what they are supposed to be doing. If you are having trouble with any of your staff on their execution, try some the techniques we discussed to see if it helps to improve the overall productivity of your company or department.

Chapter Pearls

- Control the whirlwind (11:00 Rule)
- Monitor execution by taking minutes
- Don't be a meeting tourist
- Develop and follow through on weekly commitments
- Complete your action items
- Carry a notebook and write things down
- Don't assume; monitor through 2/4/6 programs
- Track your execution score

| 4 |

Tools, Tips, and Techniques for a MOLE

A MOLE must have a set of tools in their tool kit that are reliable and can be used consistently. These are tools with which you can teach others. They will be able to predict in a given situation how you will think and what tools you will use to solve the problem. The following are tools you can use.

Trouble and the MOLE

All people and companies run into trouble from time to time. The effect of trouble on you emotionally comes down to how you think about it. A MOLE views trouble not in a negative way, but rather as an opportunity to excel and problem solve. If it is a problem the MOLE employee caused themselves inadvertently, it is an opportunity to show integrity, own up to it, and solve the issue. Overall, it's important to remember if there were no trouble in businesses there would be no need for leaders. Leadership is all about the handling of trouble, resolving issues, and working with high professionalism and integrity. MOLE employees are never afraid of trouble—it is simply another opportunity.

MOLEs Never Get Angry

Anger has no place in business; it has no place in human communication at all. The image of a red-faced employee with veins bulging in their neck, raising their voice, yelling and pounding the table is simply unacceptable. It breaks communication down, making other employees resistant to bringing any problems or discussion to the individual with anger problems. Anger is used by an individual or a leader when they simply do not have the tools to communicate properly in a given situation. They become frustrated and tend to blame other people for their inability to handle the situation. They stop listening when they get angry, demanding or using intimidation to persuade.

MOLEs instinctually understand this and do not get angry when things do not go well. They approach the problems professionally and in a way to facilitate a solution to the problem without alienating the other employees involved. When you see an employee becoming angry or raising their voice, it says more about that person and their lack of leadership ability than it does about the situation itself. People who have anger issues need to be counseled, trained, and if it does not resolve the problem, they have to be removed from the company. Anger has no place in business. MOLEs always remain calm and work professionally through their problems.

Personal MOLE Values

A MOLE has thought through their beliefs and the specific core values they hold most important. Listed below are 50 core values. MOLEs need to consider those that are most important to them. Additional core values can be found using a search engine online. Core values have areas of strength and benefit. It's important a MOLE focuses on the few that are most important to them personally. Those are the core values that you must not violate or you would be cheating yourself. As you look down through the core values, look at those that may have special meaning for you. For example, integrity and commitment are usually core values people want to emulate. Also consider, courtesy, empathy, and work ethic.

Core Values:
Adapt
Adventure
Boldness
Caring
Challenge
Collaboration
Commitment
Compassion
Consistency
Control
Courage
Creativity
Dependability
Diversity
Education
Efficiency
Elevate
Environmentalism
Evolve
Fitness
Flexibility
Good Humor
Honesty
Improvement
Innovation
Integrity
Joy
Loyalty
Motivation
Open-Mindedness
Optimism
Ownership
Partnership

Passion
Patriotism
Performance
Perseverance
Pioneer
Positivity
Professionalism
Quality
Relationships
Reliability
Respect
Responsibility
Self-Improvement
Team Spirit
Transparency
Trust
Wisdom

After you have reviewed the core values and determined which ones are most appropriate for you, look at your company's vision, mission statement, and core values. Be sure their core values match yours. This will be critical going forward. If you end up working for a company that does not have your core values, you will not be able to stay with them very long. Differences in philosophy and opinion will become regular conflict and eventually you will be forced to leave.

Work Ethic and the MOLE

Work ethic is critical. MOLEs do not shortcut processes. They do not email when a phone call would be better or use a phone call when a face-to-face is critical. The truth is when people do not have a strong work ethic or begin to cut corners it becomes very apparent to everyone around them.

A Message to Garcia

Many years ago, there was an article written by Elbert Hubbard concerning an event that occurred during the Spanish-American War in 1898. The article was written about a message that needed to be taken to General Garcia on the island of Cuba. Major Rowan who carried the message demonstrated core values including work ethic, ownership, and integrity. The article was so famous that in the 1950's many grade school students had to read it and write essays on personal qualities and initiatives. We would like you to take a few minutes and review the article, because the message that was relayed in 1899 relating to this incident is true today.

A Message to Garcia
Elbert Hubbard
1899

In all this Cuban business there is one man stands out on the horizon of my memory like Mars at perihelion.

When war broke out between Spain and the United States, it was very necessary to communicate quickly with the leader of the Insurgents. Garcia was somewhere in the mountain fastnesses of Cuba - no one knew where. No mail or telegraph could reach him. The President must secure his co-operation, and quickly.

What to do!

Someone said to the President, "There's a fellow by the name of Rowan will find Garcia for you, if anybody can."

Rowan was sent for and given a letter to be delivered to Garcia. How "the fellow by name of Rowan" took the letter, sealed it up in an oil-skin pouch, strapped it over his heart, in four days landed by night off the coast of Cuba from an open boat, disappeared into the jungle, and in three weeks came out on the other side of the island, having traversed a hostile country on foot, and having delivered his letter to Garcia, are things I have no special desire now to tell in detail. The point I wish to make is this: McKinley gave Rowan a letter to be delivered to Garcia; Rowan took the letter and did not ask, "Where is he at?"

By the Eternal! There is a man whose form should be cast in deathless bronze and the statue placed in every college in the land. It is not book-learning young men need, nor instruction about this or that, but a stiffening of the vertebrae which will cause them to be loyal to a trust, to act promptly, concentrate their energies; do the thing - "carry a message to Garcia!"

General Garcia is dead now, but there are other Garcias. No man, who has endeavored to carry out an enterprise where many hands were needed, but has been well-nigh appalled at times by the imbecility of the average man - the inability or unwillingness to concentrate on a thing and do it.

Slipshod assistance, foolish inattention, dowdy indifference, and half-hearted work seem the rule; and no man succeeds, unless by hook or crook, or threat, he forces or bribes other men to assist him; or mayhap, God in His goodness performs a miracle, and sends him an Angel of Light for an assistant.

You, reader, put this matter to a test: You are sitting now in your office- six clerks are within your call. Summon any one and make this request: "Please look in the encyclopedia and make a brief memorandum for me concerning the life of Corregio."

Will the clerk quietly say, "Yes, sir," and go do the task?

On your life, he will not. He will look at you out of a fishy eye, and ask one or more of the following questions:

Who was he?
Which encyclopedia?
Where is the encyclopedia?
Was I hired for that?
Don't you mean Bismarck?
What's the matter with Charlie doing it?
Is he dead?
Is there any hurry?
Shan't I bring you the book and let you look it up yourself?
What do you want to know for?

And I will lay you ten to one that after you have answered the questions, and explained how to find the information, and why you want it, the clerk will go off and get one of the other clerks to help him find Garcia - and then come back and tell you there is no such man. Of course I may lose my bet, but according to the Law of Average, I will not.

Now if you are wise you will not bother to explain to your "assistant" that Corregio is indexed under the C's, not in the K's, but you will smile sweetly and say, "Never mind," and go look it up yourself. And this incapacity for independent action, this moral stupidity, this infirmity of the will, this unwillingness to cheerfully catch hold and lift, are the things that put pure socialism so far into the future. If men will not act for themselves, what will they do when the benefit of their effort is for all?

A first mate with knotted club seems necessary; and the dread of getting "the bounce" Saturday night holds many a worker in his place.

Advertise for a stenographer, and nine times out of ten who apply can neither spell nor punctuate - and do not think it necessary to.

Can such a one write a letter to Garcia?

"You see that bookkeeper," said the foreman to me in a large factory.

"Yes, what about him?"

"Well, he's a fine accountant, but if I'd send him to town on an errand, he might accomplish the errand all right, and, on the other hand, might stop at four saloons on the way, and when he got to Main Street, would forget what he had been sent for."

Can such a man be entrusted to carry a message to Garcia?

We have recently been hearing much maudlin sympathy expressed for the "down-trodden denizen of the sweat shop" and the "homeless wanderer searching for honest employment," and with it all often go many hard words for the men in power.

Nothing is said about the employer who grows old before his time in a vain attempt to get frowsy ne'er-do-wells to do intelligent work; and his long patient striving with "help" that does nothing but loaf when his back is turned. In every store and factory there is a constant weeding-out process going on. The employer is constantly sending away "help" that have shown their incapacity to further the interests of the business, and others are being taken on. No matter how good times are, this sorting continues, only if times are hard and work is scarce, this sorting is done finer - but out and forever out, the incompetent and unworthy go. It is the survival of the fittest. self-interest prompts every employer to keep the best-those who can carry a message to Garcia.

I know one man of really brilliant parts who has not the ability to manage a business of his own, and yet who is absolutely worthless to anyone else, because he carries with him constantly the insane suspicion that his employer is oppressing, or intending to oppress, him. He can not give orders, and he will not receive them. Should a message be given him to take to Garcia, his answer would probably be, "Take it yourself."

Tonight this man walks the streets looking for work, the wind whistling through his threadbare coat. No one who knows him dare employ him, for he is a regular firebrand of discontent. He is impervious to reason, and the only thing that can impress him is the toe of a thick-soled No. 9 boot.

Of course I know that one so morally deformed is no less to be pitied than a physical cripple; but in your pitying, let us drop a tear, too, for the men who are striving to carry on a great enterprise, whose working hours are not limited by the whistle, and whose hair is fast turning white through the struggle to hold the line in dowdy indifference, slipshod imbecility, and the heartless ingratitude which, but for their enterprise, would be both hungry and homeless.

Have I put the matter too strongly? Possibly I have; but when all the world has gone a-slumming I wish to speak a word of sympathy for the man who succeeds - the man who, against great odds, has directed the efforts of others, and, having succeeded, finds there's nothing in it: nothing but bare board and clothes. I have carried a dinner-pail and worked for a day's wages, and I have also been an employer of labor, and I know there is something to be said on both sides. There is no excellence, per se, in poverty; rags are no recommendation; and all employers are not rapacious and high-handed, any more than all poor men are virtuous. My heart goes out to the man who does his work when the "boss" is away, as well as when he is home. And the man who, when given a letter for Garcia, quietly takes the missive, without asking any idiotic questions, and with no lurking intention of chucking it into the nearest sewer, or of doing aught else but deliver it, never gets "laid off," nor has to go on strike for higher wages. Civilization is one long anxious search for just such individuals. Anything such a man asks will be granted; his kind is so rare that no employer can afford to let him go. He is wanted in every city, town, and village - in every office, shop, store and factory. The world cries out for such; he is needed, and needed badly—the man who can

Carry a message to Garcia.

Major Rowan was a MOLE. His leaders were able to trust him to act promptly and complete the task at hand without having to micromanage him. Companies are looking for and need an entire team of Major Rowans, a team of MOLEs.

Personal Time Study by the MOLE

Years ago, Dr. Johnson's management style was quite different. He had not developed the concept of the MOLE. He accepted other people's problems and did their work for them. The whirlwind controlled his life. There were so many small day-to-day issues he had to solve, he found it very difficult to get any of the major projects he was working on completes. He finally began to ask himself three questions:

1. Was his day perfect?

The answer was clearly no, the whirlwind was controlling everything.

2. What exactly was the problem?

Here he was forced to sit down and study the issue. As a boy growing up on a farm, Dr. Johnson liked to spend time laying in the grass looking at the sky and thinking about different things. He took a blue pen and any time that he spent planning for the future or thinking about improving things was considered "blue time." He marked the calendar as such during those hours. On the farm, there was time that he just had to do the daily work, such as gathering eggs and feeding the cows. This was standard "green" work. On a farm, green is good. It was good work he was doing.

As he progressed in his professional life, he would go back and look at his day. He noted everything he did and any time there was just standard work that needed to get done, for example review of contracts or writing a client letter, he marked his calendar as "green" time during those hours. Going back to the farm, if an issue came up on the farm he had to take care of within the next few hours or ensure it was done before the end of the day that was very important and changed my direction, he considered this yellow. Therefore, any of those issues that came up during the workday, he marked the calendar in yellow. Red time was a dire emergency on the farm, pigs got out and he had to drop everything and run and get them reorganized again. Another example would be if the cattle were out of water and he had to immediately get down there and get the pump started to make sure they had water to drink. Red time on his job today is an angry client who must be dealt with immediately or an employee issue that requires his immediate intervention.

He marked his calendar with these four colors. Each day he tracked exactly what he was doing and the time. At the end of the first few days, he noticed his time was almost always yellow or red, there was very little green or blue. This clearly defined the problem; the whirlwind was controlling him.

3. What had he done about it?

Dr. Johnson began to carefully break down each issue and ask himself, what can be done about this problem? This was when the concept of bringing a solution with a problem, which you will read about in more depth later, was first starting to form. As he applied this concept in his professional environment, he identified the first issue was many of his managers would bring problems to him, drop the problem on his desk, and leave without bringing a solution with their problem. It was a tendency for employees to defer to him for answers and solutions. It disrupted his schedule and he began to ask them when they did this, "How would you handle this, what is your recommendation?" These were all smart people and frequently they had their own ideas, and most of them were good. They had the solutions in their heads, they just were not challenged historically with providing a recommendation. Occasionally he may have had a little different opinion, but for the most part the managers had a good handle on the proper next step. Therefore, he started a habit of asking them to bring solutions with their problems and to simply let him know about the issue so he did not have to spend time solving the problem or writing letters they could be writing. His days then began to improve. He continued to look at each breakdown in his day and how the whirlwind controlled that aspect of it. Eventually he created the 11:00 Rule which allows individuals to focus on their work without interruption until 11:00 a.m. It is Dr. Johnson's advice that all employees and MOLEs in particular do time studies to look at exactly how you are interrupted and where your day goes. Are you using the 11:00 Rule? Are you being taken away by the whirlwind in unnecessary areas? Before you can answer all three questions and develop the perfect day, you have to know and define a perfect day for yourself.

The Perfect Day

An exercise we recommend and perform ourselves on a regular basis is the concept of "the perfect day." Take a moment and imagine in your mind what the "perfect day" at work would be like. Exactly what time would you get up? What would you do next? Make coffee? Have breakfast? Exercise? Exactly how long will it take you to get ready for work? In your perfect day there is no rushing, so what time do you need to get up in order to have plenty of time for all the things you want to do before you leave to go to work? When you get to work, what does your desk look like? Is it cluttered with a lot of papers or very well organized and clean? You will get to work knowing exactly what your project will be when you walk into your office. What do you do then? Do you get a cup of coffee? Say hello to a few friends at work? Do you set up your 11:00 rule so that you can begin to focus entirely on the projects you truly want to work on?

All days have interruptions, so in your "perfect day" how will you handle these interruptions? How do you quickly work your way through them so that you can accomplish all of the things that you want to get done? In your "perfect day," do you do any traveling for the company? What meetings will you attend in your perfect day and how will you participate? Will you bring your lunch, or will you leave the building for lunch? What will you eat? How long will you work in the afternoon? What time will you leave? Will your desk be perfectly clean and organized? What time will you get home? What are your plans for the evening? Will you go to dinner or a movie with friends?

It is helpful that you have in mind how a "perfect day" would operate. Perfect days can vary for each day of the week. Complete time studies to see where your time goes and how much of the time is taken up by the whirlwind. You will be able to see areas that you can improve because they are under your control. At other times, you may need to talk to your supervisor to see if you can alter your job in some way to make your life easier and to get yourself closer to a "perfect day".

We should all have a "perfect day" in mind. Also have a "perfect week" and a "perfect month." This time includes all of the meetings that you want to attend, and some travel that you like to do for the work and personally during a week and month. The main thing is that it should include some handling of the whirlwind along the way so that you feel you are personally in control of your life. Expect the unexpected to occur, so plan for it. That is the key.

If you are to be happy in life, to achieve the goals you personally want to achieve, you must be happy, satisfied, and in control. These techniques of designing the perfect day, week, or month and having your own personal strategic plan will help you achieve all of these goals. If you can execute, the results are truly amazing.

Seat Belt Concept: How to Maintain Composure

A few years ago, we were in a heated meeting between a director and a psychiatrist who was hostile to the way that we handle mental health. Our director is known for her high integrity and is extremely passionate about what she does. Our director was deeply involved and heavily invested in the program with this client. The psychiatrist was openly attacking our program and suggesting that we were mistreating our patients. Our director quickly interrupted him. She was raising her voice and was raising herself out of her chair across the table from the psychiatrist. Having been interrupted, the psychiatrist became even more angry and started to raise his voice because he wasn't done talking yet. He had more points he wanted to make. Our director wanted to counter every point he made and virtually every sentence he uttered. The two became quite heated and the atmosphere in the meeting had broken down. The client eventually stopped the meeting because neither side was going to give in. He agreed with our director because she had made her point forcefully and correctly. She clearly convinced the client's management team at the meeting about the correctness of the mental health care. We talked to her after the meeting and suggested that usually it is better to let your opponent get all of their negative comments off their chest without interrupting, and sit quietly in your chair as if you had a seatbelt on. Once individuals are done talking and have exhausted all of their issues, you then should be able to correct the misunderstanding and move forward to provide clarity to the situation.

A week or two after that meeting Dr. Johnson received in the mail a gift from the director, which was a seatbelt. It included a note that said she would always remember to wear her seatbelt in future meetings. It is proudly displayed to this day. Remember, stay calm, wear your seatbelt, and let the opponent get all their ammunition fired before you start to correct their misunderstanding.

Agreeing with a "Crazy Person"

Leaders that frequently yell and scream to get their staff to do what they want have very few leadership skills. Occasionally you will run into people in a leadership position, sometimes a client, who is a screamer. It may be due to something that you actually have done incorrectly, and they feel they have the right to verbally abuse you or your staff concerning this issue. The best way to handle someone who yells and screams is to agree until they calm down.

Generally, people can only continue to yell and raise their voice for a short period if you are not disagreeing with them. If you are agreeing with them, then they tend to quiet down. Here is the key. It may be you have done nothing wrong, it is simply their perception, and yet you still have to agree with them. You do not have to agree you have done anything wrong, you need to agree that you understand why they would feel the way they feel. For example, suppose you have a client who believes you are not fulfilling all of your hours in a given contract. They begin to raise their voice, threaten to fire you from the contract, and suggest they are not getting their money's worth. You know they have been getting all of their hours, but your worker has been flexing shortened hours one week with longer hours the next week to ensure all of the work is completed. The way to approach it is to say, "Oh, I certainly agree, and that would upset me. I completely understand why you are concerned about this. I totally agree with you. I would be upset about that too. I understand." You keep going until they finally quiet down. Once they quiet down, then you can slowly begin to point out all of the hours in fact have been filled and that they really are getting their money's worth. You can educate them that you are doing it in a way that is more cost effective for them. Remember the client does not always care about your situation; they care about their situation. You should be helpful, not accusatory.

Let's say you clearly have made a mistake. There is no question about it. Then you simply agree with them. That was inadequate. You should not have made that mistake. You will work to not repeat the mistake. You agree this was mishandled. You will make it better. They can only be angry for so long if you are not disagreeing with them. Use this technique of agreeing with a crazy person. We call them "crazy" because they are yelling and screaming. There is no place for that. Even if a person makes a mistake, there is no reason to yell or raise your voice.

Bring a Solution with the Problem

As you go through your daily work you may come across problems you should pass on to your superiors. Be sure you have thought your way through the problem and have a recommended solution. Then, present the problem to the supervisor along with your recommended solution. The supervisor may take your suggestion, or they may recommend a different course of action. In any event, they will recognize you are a strategic thinker and you are working hard to try to understand the best way to manage this particular problem. MOLEs bring a solution with the problem. If you do not have any idea what the solution is, simply tell your supervisor and together you will come up with one.

Bright Shiny Things

Bright shiny things are exciting concepts to the individual and capture their attention. The concept of bright shiny things becomes relevant when you have an employee who gets caught up in trends, drama, or is easily distracted.

A bright shiny thing is something no one in the company has seen as a problem in the past. No one has identified this as an issue needing addressed. However, bright shiny things are so exciting the employee is ready to spend a major portion of their time focused entirely on solving the issue that was never a problem.

An example of this was a senior employee who attended a conference and learned prisons need to be prepared to deliver babies onsite. While we had no contracts in prisons, just county jails, the employee interpreted this to mean we needed to have the tools and instruments to deliver babies. It had never been a problem for our company. The concept was so interesting and exciting that the employee began to focus their energy and time on the project.

Every industry has its own nuances, so for those of you who are not familiar with corrections, jails and prisons are very different. For the sake of the story the point to understand is that typically patients in jails are there short-term—less than one year. Prison patients, however, are incarcerated for extended periods of time, and therefore have to offer many more on-site resources than short-term jails.

When you find yourself wondering if you are getting distracted by bright shiny things, you need to start talking to your supervisor. Tell them why you feel this is a problem. What evidence supports this? Have you consulted with any other experts within the organization that this problem needs time spent on a solution? You should be prepared to be coached through understanding how to ensure the issue is a true problem needing to be solved and not something that just sounds good. Tread carefully when you experience this because you do not want to become discouraged from attempting to bringing problems and solutions, but to protect everyone's time, you do need to be sure the problem needs to be solved. Then, help them develop a timeline for implementation based on the need. Make more of an effort to check in on their status with the task at hand. You want to ensure progress and focus.

Rabbit Holes

Rabbit holes are the multiple things that follow a bright shiny thing. In the original example mentioned above, the high-ranking employee's bright shiny thing was delivering babies in corrections. The rabbit hole was researching all the equipment, training, and policies that were "needed" as a result.

Another example is if you were to ask a person to update a policy that indicates it is expected that employees will arrive at work on time, but before they update the policy, the person independently decides they need to have a different font and a different font size to use across all policies in the company. Before they can choose a font and a font size, they decide it is important to research the most easily read font type and the size of the font to have a reason to change it—remember, no one has asked for this to be changed or complained about the current font or font size. Hours could have been spent on these random side thoughts when the organization has been operating just fine for possibly years using the original font and size.

In an attempt to circle back to updating the policy, the individual has now learned through researching readable fonts and font sizes that there is an educational standard for grammar and language that should be used for most of the U.S. population to read, even though no one has complained about policies being written in a way that does not make sense. Now the font size, font style, and the grammar in the policies all need to be updated across the entire company. It is important to note, however, no time has been spent and no update has been made to the one single policy that started this rabbit hole—that employees are expected to arrive at work on time. Through the hours and days wasted, employees continue to arrive late to work and no retraining or enforcement can be done by supervisors due to a lack of policy support.

Like bright shiny things, rabbit holes are massive distractions that may suck an entire team of individuals down a rabbit hole (think of the rabbit hole in *Alice in Wonderland*). Rather than a few hours that may be wasted from time to time looking at a bright shiny thing and then discounting it, rabbit holes may suck up days, resources, and other people

Another example of this would be if a person sees a poster for the employee assistance program (EAP) on the wall and tells their supervisor they think the poster should be removed due to a recent traumatic event that occurred in the facility (because we work in health care, this could be due to a heart attack or suicide). The employee thought EAP posters could be triggering. Removing the EAP poster was the bright shiny thing, and the solution to the possible problem lacks research and data.

The manager may agree that seeing that poster may trigger people at the location to remember the event and have a version of post-traumatic stress disorder. The manager gets caught up in the bright shiny thing, does not ask for data, approves posters be taken down, and then notifies other locations to do the same.

Nurses spend time taking down posters for the EAP across multiple locations, and a request is sent into human resources to stop sending out the program fliers due to the risk of PTSD. A member of human resources discontinues the process without telling anyone, and it is not until months later when a site needs to use the program that this issue is brought back up. Hundreds of facility locations and numerous departments are now stuck in a rabbit hole based on a bright shiny thing one person thought might someday become a problem—but never has been before and no data suggests it ever will be.

The entire decision-making rabbit hole would later be audited to learn that it came from one thought that one person had, and not due to any actual instances of post-traumatic stress disorder. The person even agreed maybe it was not necessary to remove them, but they were sitting at their desk one day looking at the poster and thinking about it. Now, teams across multiple locations must get new posters from human resources ASAP and monitor the reposting of a poster that should have never been taken down in the first place. This is another lesson why it is important for MOLE leaders to ask what evidence the individual has related to the identified problem they want to solve. Also, managers should ensure the person who is championing the change is aware of and can explain why the posters (or process) was being done the way it was in the first place. Communication is key.

Solutions without Problems

The problem with bright shiny things and rabbit holes is they demonstrate what we refer to as "solutions without problems." As a MOLE you will need to watch for this in yourself constantly.

Sometimes, when you first start instituting "bringing a solution with your problem," you will find yourself eager to bring solutions, even if there is no problem. Following the earlier flow of bright shiny things turning into rabbit holes, we return to the example of bringing a solution when there is no problem which occurred at our organization when a high-ranking strategic thinker attended a conference. Conference attendees ranged from correctional health care workers to prison and jail leadership.

The interesting thing about prisons is that men and women are housed separately. The entire discussion was focused on getting the tools at the women's facilities to prepare health care staff for delivering babies. They needed personal protective equipment for staff to wear, items to clip or tie off the umbilical cord, and several other things.

Our employee immediately understood we did not have the tools to do this in the jail facilities—the bright shiny thing. She began thinking of how to tailor this solution to the jails, which are a mix of male and female patients. She left the conference and began to contact vendors for equipment pricing, determine how many sites had females, and what training would look like, especially because in the jails health care workers may not be there all the time, so she believed officers should be trained as well—the rabbit hole.

Finally, this employee determined it was time to start drafting a policy on delivering babies—the solution without a problem. At this time, she had to get the policy reviewed by the CEO who said, "Wait, we do not deliver babies in jails." Through further discussion, the high-ranking employee realized that the CEO was correct—jails do not deliver babies, they send the patients to the hospital to deliver. You see it is easy to get carried away with how to change a practice based on their identified problem and their eagerness to change everything at the organization that relates to this solution. However, as a MOLE you must be sure that this is a problem that needs solved.

The program was working as it stood and the entire issue stopped right there during that conversation. This was a solution to a problem that did not exist. As you continue reading through the next sections, refer to this story as it also relates to bright shiny things (delivering babies in corrections) that can turn into a rabbit hole (research, effort, wasted time).

Final Thoughts

MOLE employees have learned the ability of great communication, complete execution of duties, and composure under stress. When they have a problem that must be presented to their supervisor, they always bring a solution or a recommendation. When you have achieved these things, you will truly be on the road to becoming a MOLE.

Chapter Pearls

- See problems as opportunities
- Stay calm; do not express anger
- Know your values and live them
- Work hard
- Take initiative and ownership over tasks (A Message to Garcia)
- Think through your perfect day
- Maintain composure (seat belt concept)
- Agree with a "crazy" person
- Bring a solution with the problem
- Do not go for "bright shiny things"
- Do not go down a rabbit hole or develop solutions without problems

MOLE LEADERSHIP

| 5 |

The MOLE Leader

Second Level of Leadership/Team Leader

After you have learned how to lead yourself, you may be promoted to what is known as a team leader. A team leader is a person who by the nature of their intelligence and work ethic can be a leader to people directly around them. This is usually someone like a health services administrator (HSA) or a director in the corporate office that has all of their employees in the corporate office they can see on a regular basis. This person has the personal skills to guide and teach one on one. They are respected by those people with whom they work shoulder-to-shoulder, and they get involved in recognizing, disciplining, hiring, and firing. They have taken complete ownership of their department. This of course requires a different set of leadership skills. For this position, one must learn labor law, OSHA regulations, corporate policies relating to hiring and firing, recognition, and discipline. Anyone in the position of a team leader will need leadership training in all the new skillsets and behaviors they will need to demonstrate.

Third Level of Leadership/Advanced MOLE Leadership

The third level of leadership is the advanced leader. This leader requires all of the skill sets of the team leader but in addition must have the ability to think strategically to predict problems before they develop and resolve them. They must develop monitoring systems that closely watch the productivity of employees and direct reports that are many miles away from them. This is not easy and requires training and skills far beyond that of a team leader. The biggest failing we see in advanced leaders is the inability to appropriately monitor their direct reports. This results in problems developing in a distant site without their being aware of it. Eventually this causes a crisis, which forces them to change their schedule and interferes with the normal flow of their work.

In one example, we had a tenured leader with a high performing direct report. The leader promoted the direct report to a mid-level manager and praised the individual on communication and reliability. Months after the promotion, the direct report requested to work remotely and move several states away. Due to the person's work ethic and performance, the leader not only approved the move, but encouraged the organization to help pay for it.

Shortly after that move, the leader started noticing that the direct report was having trouble sending work to the leader on time. Excuses were accepted and past performance outshined the current behavior so no action was taken timely. Finally the leader decided to do an audit of the direct report's territory. The themes of 1) no communication, 2) lack of contact, and 3) not knowing the name of their contact with our organization were startling.

Because of the leader's delay in monitoring and addressing behaviors, we learned too late in the process that the direct report was not effectively working as a remote employee. The direct report lacked the ability to set a schedule and hold himself accountable without oversight.

After the audit results were brought to the direct report's attention, it was shared that the home whirlwind became distracting. The direct report was making quick trips to the store and doing laundry when there was work and travel to do.

From what we have experienced, the whirlwind starts with stealing fifteen minutes here and there and evolves into reduced hours working due to increasing home responsibilities. The work from home position is only successfully done when it comes to the right person in the right role. Approvals, as a result, should be to try for a temporary period of time and include intense monitoring, especially in the beginning.

This was another shortfall we learned late in the process. The leader did not know how to effectively monitor remote staff. Following this situation, we were able to intervene and get the leader additional training through setting up monitoring systems for her team. This is started through ensuring the leader is aware of what job ownership is and how it relates to the work the direct report will be doing, and pairing it with the direct report's ability to complete tasks through self-motivation and structure.

Advanced MOLE leadership is the ability to be friendly with all direct reports without being best friends. It is the ability to develop a relationship based on trust and respect, even when you do not work side by side with the individual—they could be states away—when they are struggling. This means MOLE leaders have the ability to honestly analyze the productivity of people without becoming involved with those direct report's personal lives.

Ineffective leaders who cross into personal boundaries and become friends with staff may unconsciously or consciously allow staff to underperform, or make excuses for low productivity. This can bring up claims of favoritism. Advanced MOLE leaders understand the reasons behind the rules so when a variation develops in a situation, an advanced MOLE leader can come up with a solution that makes sense. Advanced MOLE leaders have solutions with the problems they present to their superiors, and MOLEs are comfortable being responsible for everything. They know where to go to get the resources to assist them and help them. An advanced leader develops systems and has new concepts to improve and help the company. These are then presented at the routine meetings and can be used to improve and change the entire company from time to time.

Building a Team

As you become a MOLE leader and begin to look at your staff, it is likely you will have pre-existing staff with experience and tenure. You will need to work closely with your inherited staff to provide clear communication as you begin to train them on new (possibly more restrictive) expectations that they have not historically have had to work under. For example, it may have been common for employees to show up whenever they wanted and leave when they felt they were done for the day. In a MOLE Leadership environment, schedules are consistent and planned in most cases. Therefore, the MOLE leader will need to speak with inherited staff about what is occurring, find out the reason behind what they are doing, express the desire to change the expectations, and provide a timeline of adjusting to it. A MOLE leader recognizes change is hard on individuals and there should be a transitional period to help the staff get up to speed on new expectations—especially when the person liked the old way of doing things. Paired with the ongoing training and support of the MOLE leadership system, these inherited individuals will bring experience, skill and new energy to the team. It has been common to hear comments such as, "I've never felt so supported before," or "This is the first time my supervisor has asked me that question."

Through clear communication and examples of the ultimate goals, the inherited staff will decide if they are willing to adjust their practices or if they would prefer to search for a different company culture more in line with their personal goals. Do not feel obligated to retain inherited individuals who are not performing at your level of expectation.

It is also likely a leader will have to hire employees to build their team. Without focusing on the specifics of the hiring process, it is necessary to understand the big picture of who you want to hire. When you have an open position for any reason, take time to consider the type of individual who would be successful in this role. What type of skills do you want them to be strong in so value will be added to the organization and tasks will be done well? What type of skills are you willing and able to train/teach them on if they have less experience?

Does the role require certain certifications or specific hours? Then pair that with personality tendencies and/or motivational factors discussed next in the book that you think would be beneficial or challenging for the role. A vision for the employee starts to form in your head prior to reviewing any applications. This is your baseline from which to start to compare applicants.

Chapter Pearls

- Take ownership over yourself and your department
- Accept learning and training opportunities as a team leader
- Honestly analyze the productivity of people as an advanced leader
- Beware of crossing personal/professional boundaries with employees
- Lead with clear communication and reasonable transparency

| 6 |

Personality Factors for the MOLE Leader

As we see the progression of the work-life balance trend enter an increasing number of organizations, we are also beginning to see the importance of understanding how each individual differs at their core. The concepts of personality and motivation stem far deeper than an association of traits and obvious differences between individuals and requires a mature review of unconscious personal preference biases.

We recommend you use a system for personality evaluation to assist your staff in understanding what motivates them and the people with whom they work. Our company uses a free online test called 16 Personalities (which can be accessed through www.16personalities.com) and each employee is categorized by the system into 1 of 16 different types. It follows a similar structure as the Meyers-Briggs test, and then further shares rankings based on individual traits. As you progress through the chapter you may notice four-letter indicators for a personality type. These are intentionally left in to allow readers to relate the personality test we use to the one they may actively use which also assigns letters. For example, an ISFJ for 16 Personalities is a Defender. However, Meyers-Briggs simply calls it an ISFJ personality. Furthermore, while the letters indicate similar characteristics across personality test brands, they may be assigned a different official name depending on the test you use. Do not get overly focused on the letters. Choose a personality test and keep it consistent so you can start to see variations in humans. No matter the test, the general concepts still apply.

Of note, personality testing should never be used to make a hiring decision. For example, there should never be statements such as, "Do not put a Defender (ISFJ) in this role," or "I only want a Consul (ESFJ) hired" or "All Protagonists (ENFJ) are liars." What a hiring manager can do is use the information from the test and the information provided in the interview to ask follow up questions regarding the role. The applicant is seeking a role to generate income and be satisfied in their position, the hiring manager is interviewing to find a person who will be willing to complete the tasks successfully and a company culture fit to avoid unnecessary conflict or frustration from the person or their new peers.

For example, you are hiring for a transcription role and their results indicate they are highly extraverted. You, as the employer, know the person will be sitting in a cubicle location and the tasks of the position require a quiet location with limited staff interaction. Because of the personality test, the manager can be prompted to explain, in more depth than usual, that the role is isolated. It may even prompt the manager to show the location of the office to ensure the person feels they will be successful in that role. If they are, it is a very transparent interviewing process, and if they are not okay with it, the manager saved them from resigning to come work for a place that was not collaborative enough for them. Interviews are a two-way street with each person (the interviewee and the interviewer) deciding if they want to enter into the employment relationship based on information provided and discussed.

Commonly when we provide that example, we have a hiring manager who will ask, "Why can't I just tell them no if they are highly extraverted and the role is highly introverted?" This is because the tests are not designed for hiring, and assumptions can lead to skewed results or inaccurate predications. We do believe if you are interviewing multiple candidates and one is highly extraverted, for example, scenarios of this will come out in their interview. Extraverted individuals will likely have stories of engagement that highlight their preference to interact whereas more introverted individuals may naturally focus on their independent habits. By way of communicating with the applicant and comparing them to other applicants, it is most likely you will identify someone that is a good fit for the role assigned, whether or not that has to do with being highly extraverted. More specifically, if one candidate shares they prefer to work in a group setting, all of their examples share experiences interacting with others, and the thing they're most looking forward to about coming to the company is all the new faces they'll meet or clients they'll interact with—you'll know they are probably not the individual you want to place in an isolated transcription desk job. However, that does not mean you are excluding them due to extraversion. Introverts are also social too; you are choosing a different candidate who prefers isolated tasks more.

We have taken time to review and understand 16 personalities from our own interpretation and application. You will need to do the same for whatever personality system you choose to pursue and/or purchase. There are groups of people who are focused naturally on data, those who are more creative thinkers, and still others who are great at consistent routine. Of the group, there are people who become frustrated when they are unbalanced in their role and tend to take things too personally, or lash out at others, or feel they are the only one pulling their weight. All of this is mentioned as tendencies of personalities you can use as a tool in the process before and ongoing in the employment process.

Not every person will agree with personality testing, they may feel it is too invading or, more commonly, declinations come from people who think this is similar to a poor horoscope that can apply to anyone. From using it as long as we have now, we have found ways to overcome this by discussing preferences and tendencies with the individuals so they may recognize their own preferences. As they come across difficulties with coworker interactions, we discuss their coworkers' tendencies and preferences to see if a more positive outcome can occur with a different strategy. Usually, trying it one time is all it takes to help this type of individual understand the goal is positive collaboration, not critical judgement. We want to foster an atmosphere of support for our differences and focus on the tasks at hand. It would not be wise to intentionally match people based on similar tendencies, because the project may lose some creativity and innovation potential by only choosing like-minded individuals. That type of behavior is not the point of personality testing. Personality testing is not a shortcut to avoid getting to know people or a tool of manipulation; it is a way to remind ourselves to look at ourselves first, consider the receiver of the information and communicate in a way that attempts to make the message the most clear.

When selecting your personality testing site, there are free sites which can benefit smaller organizations such as the test above, but there are also options to purchase additional information that may provide even more insight to tendencies. Start slow and identify an individual who can read through the information and present it in a way that is all-inclusive and motivating to employees. Personality testing should never be used to hire, fire, or discipline. All of that should be the result of experience and specific behaviors.

Chapter Pearls

- Use a system for personality evaluation
- Do not use personality evaluations to hire, fire, discipline, etc.

| 7 |

Motivational Factors for the MOLE Leader

Next, we talk about determining an employee's motivation for being at or joining your organization. The subject of motivation should not be framed as an attempt to only learn why the person thinks your organization is great (assuming they do). What you want to know is: what motivates this person to show up every day? This gets us back to the earlier discussion of the six gardens of life. Any one factor can be so powerful that it makes other factors (or gardens) less important at the time. Is it a financial need, it is an internal drive to reach a certain career aspiration, or is it a personal cause? There can be a balance of reasons and changing motivations throughout a person's career but knowing their motivation will help you work with them.

You must understand people have certain personal goals and ideas about their career. It may be they are perfectly happy, and just want to work another 10 or 15 years and then retire out of their present job. That is okay. On the other hand, someone may be in a position that they want to constantly grow and move up the corporate ladder. That is okay, too. It helps to know what their personal goals are because you may be able to put them on a track to help them achieve their goals. If the company does not have the position or the career track they are really interested in, you may be able to assist them when it comes time to move on to another job or another career. This may happen if an employee is in school for a professional degree such as nursing, They simply have to let you know how you can assist and help in their personal growth.

If you have an employee who is there for their financial need, that is okay. Recognize this is a person who may be further motivated by overtime opportunities or promotion. They will be less likely to want time off to go home (unpaid). Each person will be different based on how they are moving through their life. Reviewing the section of the Gardens of Life within this text will assist with this as well. But beware: those who are focused on the paycheck may be more apt to fall for the zombie mentality and viral conversations. You can work to invest them in the company culture and mission while fulfilling their needs in their life.

We used to have an employee who was wonderful at her job but wanted to advance to a higher position when she was only two months on the job. She was career driven and smart enough to learn the concepts. Unfortunately, she did not have the experience or related education. She did not want to do any additional training and felt entitled to get a higher position quickly. We would talk often and because of this, we suggested she consider working with us to develop a plan with our organization to get her where she wanted over the course of a couple years. She declined, wanting the promotion sooner. Because her career goals did not align with our organization's growth plans for her (which included a certain skillset and knowledge in higher positions), we were unable to save her.

Ultimately she resigned on positive terms to join an organization that hired her in at the level she wanted. Shortly after, we became her sounding board for dealing with leadership issues at her new job. She was having issues with the missing skill set and task knowledge we had previously discussed when she wanted a promotion within our organization. She was in over her head and started realizing she might not have been ready for that point in her career. Unfortunately, she did not stay at that organization for a long period of time.

Those who are motivated to work because of an internal, personal cause can be some of the most inspirational people at organizations. These are people who are not working because they have to; they work because they want to. However, they can scare leaders due to their ability to quit and move on to a new cause. We experienced this situation when a manager once told us he was hesitant to hire a doctor because the doctor did not financially need the job. The manager's reasoning was that hypothetically in the future, the manager was afraid the doctor would quit without notice if the doctor ever changed their mind about working. What we discussed is that when it comes down to it, anyone can leave a job. It is ideal to get to know them as employees to find out from them what makes them feel motivated and feed that drive. This is done through customizing the job tasks reasonably to fulfill the tasks and engage the worker. For example, if they want to help people and you place them in data entry, they may be skilled, but they are not long for your company. Determine if you can allow time for them to join a committee that brainstorms and implements changes for staff, or give them enough authority to field incoming issues and provide recommended solutions. Matching motivation is key while still getting the business needs completed.

Chapter Pearls

- Learn what motivates your employees
- Develop growth plans together
- Assist them to grow or exit the organization positively

| 8 |

Company Culture

You will need to get a solid understanding of your quirks as a company. What does the company culture look like and how does that compare to the type of culture an applicant wants to work within? How does the company feel the applicant will fit in given the rules of the company culture? For example, if you have an employee who shows up in a suit and tie coming to interview in an organization where everyone wears jeans or sweatpants, is this the culture the applicant wants to be in? What values does the company hold everyone to and how does that compare to the value guidelines the applicant wants to work within? For example, if a value of the company is to be professional, and the company allows the use of profanity, is that the same definition of professional the applicant is seeking?

Matching people to jobs is extremely important. You do not want a person quitting their job only to find out the new job, culture, and values are unacceptable to them. As we progress, you will learn more about the culture and values review. You will also learn ways to identify what your company culture is and what it is not. You will learn how to identify what is most important to you and how to focus on it, such as hiring MOLEs and not MOLD.

Company Culture Review

It is necessary for employers to convey their company culture during their recruiting and interviewing process. According to LHH, a talent advisory and solutions company, 89 percent of hiring failures are due to a poor company culture fit. In the interview process companies need to look for people who have the skills to do the job and the personality tendencies that fit with their unique culture. Through several months of discussions and interviews with current employees, we learned our company's culture is one where employees have the ability to collaborate, problem solve, and be personally accountable for their decisions and actions. This is not to discount several other wonderful values, but these were deemed the most important. These values are different than the ones for which we award staff within the organization (as discussed in the values review section).

These top interview values became extremely important to remember when we had an interview for a traveling nurse. The candidate would be responsible for going to multiple facilities and interacting with clients, staff, and patients. During the MOLE interview, the candidate was asked to share a time in which their task failed. The candidate proceeded to tell the group their humor sometimes got them in trouble. With a previous employer, the candidate had gone to a secure facility which required people to be buzzed in and out of rooms. To get the door open, it was necessary to announce the request via two-way radio. The candidate made a joke by announcing over the two-way radio something to the effect of "We have a code purple at door three." At other sites, the candidate would laugh and be buzzed into the next room by whoever was watching the security tapes and granting access. However, in this new facility, a code purple alerted the staff of evacuation procedures, and the location as a whole began to move patients, call out protocols, and lock down the facility. As the story ended, the candidate never explained how their behavior would change in the future. It was shared as a time the joke went bad, not as a learning opportunity to grow from and a behavior to discontinue. In the interviewer's minds, this was highly unprofessional and would not work in a company culture such as ours. It may work elsewhere, but why would we want to set this person up for failure? They had a sense of humor that would work out quite well in another company culture, but could set them up for failure in our company.

Once the group debriefed with the hiring manager, two high ranking managers brought up this story, giving very high scores, and laughing at how funny it was. The managers—our managers—had failed to understand the future repercussions that could come from this type of behavior translating into our organization. The individual was not a good fit for our company culture compared to other applicants as it related to the entire MOLE interview process (not exclusively on this one particular answer). Then, we had the job of retraining our managers to spot behaviors such as this and recognizing the future implications of moving someone forward with mismatched behavior expectations.

When it comes to building company culture, our recommendation is to not hire anger. In our experience, individuals with anger cannot collaborate. They bring problems, and often make excuses or blame others for their actions. They are MOLD. To decrease the chances of getting angry individuals hired in our organization, we created a screen out question, based off the recommendation from Mark Murphy's book *Hiring for Attitude*. We will not provide you our specific question because we are still using it successfully to this day!

To create your own individualized screen out question, you must take time to truly think about the one thing you do (or do not) want in your organization. It must be specific. When we did this, we had a team of five or more people who were all challenged with bringing ideas to the meeting. We discussed and collaborated together until we came to the final question. When you classify a value too broadly, such as "team player", any applicant will be able to tell you they are a team player. The goal is to get down to the specific need, and then create a question based around it that cannot be gamed and the answer cannot be guessed. Determining your own initial screen out question will help determine if a person is the right company culture fit for your company.

If people do not pass it, then they are screened out early in the process before any more time is wasted for them or the organization.

To attract the right individual for your company culture, companies need to ensure they have the benefits those individuals seek. Communicating a total rewards package, including the process for advancement, attracts applicants. One way to audit your own company culture is to create a committee to list out and find ways to market the benefits of the company. We did this through our Employer of Choice committee. What started as a brainstorming meeting to uplift the company culture turned into efforts to get certified as a Great Place to Work due to the satisfaction of our staff.

Once people are attracted to the company, interviewers have the responsibility not to hire them unless it is mutually beneficial. The new hires are uprooting their lives, many times stopping their income, to take a chance on what the interviewer has promised. If it does not work out due to tasks or due to personality conflicts, the interviewer should have determined that early on. Quite frankly, if we cannot deliver on promises that we've made to employees, we cannot expect them to deliver for us.

We advise interviewers and managers refrain from making promises or statements they cannot deliver on or control. One example is to not promise an applicant the hiring manager will call them back later that day. This is because the hiring manager may be busy. Failing to get the call to the applicant the day you promised may damage trust. Instead, attempt to contact the hiring manager and to ask the hiring manager to contact the applicant. Notify the applicant to call back directly if they do not hear from the hiring manager in a few days. That keeps you in the loop until the goal is fulfilled and puts some of the accountability of follow up on the applicant, too. Don't make promises you can't keep.

Values Review

Before we can discuss how to employ a workforce of MOLE employees, the organization itself must have a solid understanding of its own values that support the company's purpose, vision, and mission. A quick online search will provide a wide range of recommended values from 3 to 190 or more necessary values that businesses should consider to be the most effective and best employer. As time goes on, the recommended number of values changes based on the team's opinion that reviews them. Even the description of what a value is changes based on who is writing the article. Some companies use statements while others use terms. This can be further complicated because not every company should have the same internal values and belief systems. The values need to be in line with the intentions of the organization. It is not wise to focus an entire company culture on efficiency and responsiveness if the business is in architecture, for example. To build a proper architectural building, specific tools and resources are needed along with adequate planning time to ensure codes are met. Pushing workers to be fast would produce increased anxiety and errors. Therefore, a company culture audit is needed for whatever organization you are wanting to uphold or change.

Our organization decided to choose specific terms for values and through time, recognized we also needed to define what each value means to our specific organization. This is not something that is done by many other companies. Simply accepting the term found in a dictionary will not define what the term means to your specific organization. The value definition should be specific to the behavior you want your employees to display.

It is necessary at this point to consider the values you have internally, those you want for the organization, and values you believe the organization currently is operating under effectively. It is okay if the current workforce does not necessarily promote the values you want of them. With time and effort, they will start to display the values, or they will choose to move on from the organization. It is more important incoming workers do share the same core values. This explains the difference in top values in hiring versus those for which we use for employees. As you may recall, when we are interviewing we look for collaboration, problem solving, and accountability. We want people to come to us with these skills already mastered and exhibited. Therefore, we developed interview questions aimed at hiring for those main values. Over time, the questions have changed as we've tailored them to specific roles. What we may want in one role may not be the most important in another. For example, in the role of a lawyer, we may be looking for timeliness, collaboration, and professionalism. In the role of a frontline medical professional, we may be looking for accountability, integrity, and respectfulness. Focusing on the values allows companies to look for people who already embody these values and will naturally exhibit them in their day-to-day roles with minimal conscious effort.

Once they are on staff, we look to challenge each other to exhibit the top values of professionalism, integrity and commitment. We also reward them for the values we want to improve upon in our company culture. This results in the organization becoming an enjoyable place to work.

So after being hired into the organization, the other numerous values are used to uphold or tweak behaviors. We discuss the values annually and have collaborative discussions on writing the definitions as they relate to our organization for the next year. By way of example, in our organization the opposite of collaboration is anger, because it is uncommon for us to witness an employee working well together with others when they also feel that yelling emotionally is necessary.

Using Values

To ensure the values are not a list filed away in a folder, we developed ways to keep them relevant. Therefore, employees experience the values on a day-to-day basis. We expanded our recognition program (explained in Chapter 15), which encourages day-to-day thank you's based on values and specific instances. We also developed an end of the year award to recognize one employee in the company who most represents these values. Then, if corrections need to be made, all our constructive coaching is also focused on the values. That way, we can speak to specific behaviors employees are exhibiting with the intent to encourage or discourage the actions.

It is important a company's leadership realizes the impact of acting and living the company's culture. It cannot be done in one conversation, with little effort, and completed with an eye roll. The values are extremely important, and if the leadership team does not encourage the use and preach the need, then the frontline staff will start to view the company as untrustworthy due to their message not matching their leader's actions. This is why people write things like "corporate doesn't care" in online forums.

To get started for your organization, think about the purpose, vision, and mission and what values to accomplish this are needed. Search the internet for values and schedule a meeting with the leaders of the company. In this situation, we recommend directors and above have about a two-hour long meeting. This meeting would be set to explain the needs of your organization, show the value examples, and decide on only one to five top company values. At the current time, the definitions may be what is found commonly on an internet search or in a dictionary. They will mold to your company culture over time. Once you know the top three values, subsequent meetings may be set to add in upwards of 25 or so more—whatever your organization is comfortable with. Bringing in human resources at this point will help timeline the roll out of values and development of a communication plan for the organization. From this plan, the recruiting department should also be trained on the intentions, so they may modify their practices and screen outs so that they comply with all necessary laws and regulations.

Chapter Pearls

- Matching people to a job is a difficult skill to master
- Understand the company values you are seeking
- Communicate clearly in the interview process

| 9 |

Hiring the MOLE

To run an efficient department or organization, MOLE employees are needed. A MOLE is an individual who will make your life easier as a manager, coworker, or owner. This type of person takes personal ownership and accountability for their tasks. They are experts in their role who continue to grow professionally and who focus on solutions, rather than spending time on viral conversations. MOLE employees make lives easier by executing what they commit to and then recommend efficiencies where they can be implemented.

Preliminary Hiring Factors

With recruiting on board, it is time to determine how to get a staff of MOLE employees. Reality check: you cannot just decide one day to hire a MOLE. There are only a few ways to get a MOLE, and none of the strategies include the dated post and pray method. The post and pray method of recruiting occurs when a company posts a job opening online and then hopes that a good candidate will be looking for a job, be attracted to their ad, and apply. In most cases, MOLE employees are either grown by you or you spend time researching resumes from gainfully employed individuals and try to sway them to make a life change. When you choose to work with an employee who requires training to become an expert, it is considered an investment in their career growth. This growth occurs when a person is hired and the organization invests time and money into not only training the individual to learn the company's expectations, but also spends time and money investing in the employee's personal professional growth, creating a true expert in their field.

The research method is also called sourcing in the recruiting world and requires a massive amount of time and confidence that the person they found is the best person for the job. A manager cannot wake up one day and decide to hire someone who will work hard and be loyal to a company. As many businesses texts touch on, this process starts with knowing and being comfortable with your company culture. A manager who does not know the company culture cannot maintain or tweak the culture based upon engagement. They lack control or even an understanding of the whirlwind or personality conflicts around them. A company's culture is built on a company's reputation through marketing, community presence, and employee perceptions.

Companies must market with the intent to grow a MOLE strategically. Notice how we did not say advertise? Marketing is a way of attraction. It is a popularity contest of what company is the most attractive to join. There should be a pleasing logo, practices of low-cost marketing (think of branded giveaway items as walking billboards), and an active social media page. A few years ago your organization's industry would dictate which social media platform your company should use to communicate. Some platforms encourage posting thoughts without evidence or fact. However, platforms have a strength of getting their company brand communicated if the information shared is not too controversial. For example, in the current industry, we recommend a company having a social media page, but to have all comments restricted. It can be used as a one-sided conversation for companies to post their information as free advertising.

Typically, there is at least one person in a large organization assigned to control the messages and tailor comments based upon the social sites. There are many other social medial platforms that could benefit organizations if there is an understanding that the goal of social media is free branding and communication to attract a MOLE. MOLEs are smart—they do not need to be spoon-fed your website or a lot of details about who to call. If they want to work somewhere, they will search it online, find the application page, and wait months for interviews if they want it bad enough.

It is important to note the potential MOLE employee may not have specific history working in the industry, and even if they have a degree, it does not mean they can be placed in a position and left alone to work. A company who wants to grow MOLE employees must be prepared to mentor and train them, or the employee will leave within a year or two. MOLE employees are generally smart enough to know word of mouth and community reputation is an important part of getting a job. They do not want to get involved with potentially talking negatively about a former employer, so the reasons will be due to personal reasons, moving, time constraints, etc. They will not tell you the benefits were bland or the job bored them. Attracting a potential MOLE to apply to you is only half the battle, once they apply or reach out, companies still must recognize specific skillsets and then work to train them. If someone reaches out to your organization, even if you do not have a job open, it is a good idea to take the interview with the understanding that nothing is currently open.

The post and pray method is not a proven or ideal way to hire a MOLE, however in rare situations a MOLE will respond to a posting. This post and pray method has transpired into behavioral interviewing, personality testing, background checks, and reference checks. It seems everyone in the business world works off a model like this, and yet hiring is still a gamble. This is because MOLE employees give their employer every opportunity to keep them and satisfy their personal needs. When they feel underappreciated or want to know their worth to an outside organization, they will begin the interview process.

Sourcing

The most ideal—though also the most expensive—way to hire a MOLE is sourcing for an expert. This should be considered if time cannot be spent building work ethic and loyalty through mentoring and training over time. We would recommend going to business networking sites directly to websites of large organizations to find their top people.

Business Networking

There are business networks that are a modern-day online resume. Individuals who sign up are able to network with other people at their level in different organizations and display their experience. Organizations do not feel threatened at this point in time when their employees are on these sites, though there is nothing they can do about it even if they do not like it. This creates the perfect platform for a MOLE to let recruiters and other organizations to come to them.

For an organization seeking to find a MOLE, these sites allow anyone within the organization the ability to review gainfully employed employees, identify where they are working, and for how long. Caution should be used by managers and recruiters so as to not make biased decisions based upon protected information they learn (age, race, gender, etc.). Potential MOLEs can be contacted or the information can be used to find them on their company's website, depending on their level. When using sites in this way, be cautious about believing all of the information. Be sure to ask questions to rule out inaccuracies.

Company Websites

If a company is seeking a specific MOLE, chances are it is for an executive or specialized position. Going to the company website is a great tool to use because executive names and emails are typically displayed. Pairing the tenure information found on business networking sites will tell a recruiter or manager how bought in to the culture the person is. For example, someone who has been with an organization for 10 years most likely agrees and lives up to the expectations outlined in the company's vision and mission. This data is useful during future interviews to compare against your organization's vision and mission, and in determining how much the vision and mission of an organization means to the person.

Executive Search Firms

When needed, executive search firms do a good job of finding candidates for a company. We recommend using this as a last resource for a few reasons. First, the cost to hire one of their applicants is very, very high. Second, there are some contracts that require payment whether or not they find you a person. Third, it does not decrease your work in hiring. The executive search firms will want to know all your contacts and connections to get them started. If you fail to provide leads, the person they bring forward may be someone you had already considered. Wouldn't it be terrible if you were actively considering someone on your own, and now a search firm tries to claim they found the person? You must exhaust all your own options before you go third party. Finally, your organization will still have to do the normal screen out and interviewing. There is a place for executive search firms, but in my opinion, it is for a situation where you need a remote leader from a hard to get industry and your organization does not know where to start.

Through the years, Dr. Johnson and Dr. Moriarity have each been contacted by recruiters trying to place them with other organizations. Unfortunately, there is usually a gap between the reasons recruiters are calling and what is in it for the employee to make the life change. The intent of contacting experts in the field is to attempt to engage in a more open-door conversation as to what the employment package would be. The standard offer will not always be what the expert is looking for, but there are ways for communicating a "what would it take" conversation. Experts in high-level positions will at least consider the ability to have control over making a new company successful. If the conversation does not result in interest, the expert will surely know someone else in the field who might be worth contacting. The person may or may not be with their organization. Sharing that information with a recruiter builds the expert's network and leaves the door open for the recruiter to contact them in the future.

If the sourcing route produces a candidate, the organization should be prepared to find out what the MOLE would need to make the role successful. Experts are good at big picture and leadership, and many times they will need staff to implement their visions. Are there experts to support them that are already with the organization? Will the applicant plan to bring staff? Will staff need to be hired? A manager will need to know what they are getting into when hiring a MOLE who is already in an expert role. There is a great benefit with this, but initially there will also be an investment. Depending on the transparency of the organization, a benefit to this route is the MOLE should be expected to have improvements started within the first three months. Month one is learning the interactions of the company, month two is their communication and plan development, and month three is the beginning stages of implementation. MOLE experts are not hired for day-to-day monotonous work, nor are they hired to deal with personality conflicts. MOLE experts are individuals who are attracted to change when it is for sound reasoning and company stability. The MOLE expert should also have a balance of being highly organized, an eagerness to improve, and prioritizing logic. MOLE experts have high work ethics.

The Application

Organizations will be unable to identify a MOLE employee by the way application processes are structured. It is worth auditing your current practices for screening applicants. Ensure the process screens out what is required but does not become overly restrictive or discriminatory. You should allow for all demographics and backgrounds to apply. Understand the experience, job responsibilities as they relate to the open position, and applicant salary expectations (expectations are different from asking what they are currently making; asking what they are currently making has become a protected question and employers should refrain from this question).

If your organization must do a background check, it is best practice to wait until after an interview, however it is reasonable to promote the expectations of the role, such as checking a box that states, "I understand I must clear a background check to work in this role." The same can be done to notify applicants that a drug screen is required. Upfront notification is appreciated by applicants because it shows you are not trying to waste their time if they do not wish to continue.

The Skill Interview

Interviewing is a learned skill and not everyone is good at it, even if they think they are. When reviewing applications and preparing to interview applicants, interviewers would be wise to realize that MOLE employees will have many different personality traits, and there is no one specific thing for which to look. The fact that everyone who applies for a role has varying backgrounds and abilities will further complicate the interview process (complicate it in a good way!). Many times, the MOLE applicant can be easily outshined by lesser performing applicants due to a focus on the interviewer's feelings (their gut) rather than facts. People can misrepresent themselves in the process if questions are not specific and answers are generalized.

The intent of the skill interview is to talk to the person face-to-face, validate what is on their résumé, and discuss the job you have open. If you are new to interviewing, make sure you review a list of questions you may not ask in an interview. Some interviewers turn the interview into a social hour and unintentionally ask inappropriate questions. Interviewing is a skill and should not be misclassified as an easy conversation. In day-to-day life, it is okay to ask people where they are from, how long they have lived places, and if they are part of certain social organizations. In day-to-day life, it is perceived as friendly to ask about family and future personal plans. This is not the case for interviewing. Asking candidates about their family life can result in discrimination. Knowing someone's age can lead to feeling they are too young or too old for the job. Knowing someone has children can lead to a feeling they will be taking a lot of time off or show up to work late. Judging people based on their social affiliations can lead to religious discrimination. This is not an exhaustive list. Ignorance is not an excuse when it comes to discrimination, and your skill interview should be focused on only their ability to do the job you need to get filled. Their personal life should not be a concern, and if they bring it up, it is your job as the interviewer not to document notes on it and to redirect the interview back to the job duties.

There is no concern with oversharing about the role to give an honest depiction of what the person is getting themselves into. Show them actual manuals they will be working in or some of the systems —without disclosing confidential items—they would have to function within. Walk them around the environment and explain the culture out loud. As an interviewer it will be important not to get lost in the "sales" part of the position. If you like the person you will naturally talk and share information. The point of sharing information here, though, is to gauge their reactions to work, the people they meet, and the tasks you are talking to them about. Stay focused. See if they are reacting in a way you would want from an employee or if they offer up ideas on the spot. Look through nerves as best as you can and start to talk about the tough items. Essentially, this interview is a good time to make all of the tasks and expectations of the job and company very clear.

It is in everyone's best interest not to gloss over the tasks of a job during the interview process and instead provide real insight. This is the process of telling them what it is like on a day-to-day basis and then moving forward to talk about the challenges. Without oversharing, it is reasonable to discuss the existence of challenging personalities or processes that need refined or improved. Then discuss salary expectations. The application should have their expectation, but at this point, you know their background. Let them know what your starting point is. If they shy away from it, you have to make a judgement call if this is as far as they go or if you need to push further to negotiate. By the end of this interview, you should know if the person can or cannot do the job and if the person would accept the rate you're willing to pay.

If interviewers research personality testing and interviewing, they will learn it is generally poor practice to use personality testing as the sole decider of who to hire. We completely agree with this because it supports the "trusting your gut" style of interviewing. Just because you like the person in a two-hour interview does not mean they will make your life easier in their role. Your role and their role are most likely different, and what you will need from them in work may differ from how they interact with you as they sell themselves.

People will have varying degrees of traits that relate to things like social interaction, interacting with data, handling emotions, organizing their thoughts, and dealing with stress. Social interaction is not an indicator of friendliness. It speaks to the type of office environment you will need to place them in to get the most productivity out of them. Interview guides have misguided future applicants into preparing for interviews in a way that is unhelpful in actually matching a person's skillset and preferences to the task or job in need. Today, people say they are great at working in teams, but also great at working alone. This is due to a poor question from the interviewer. What interviewers need to know is if the person is going to be burned out and become unproductive if they are put in a noisy office with a lot of talkers, or if they will feel insecure and alone if they are working from a home office in the middle of nowhere.

The way they interact with data allows an interviewer to place them in a position that is highly structured with clear goals, or more of a spontaneous role where they need to figure things out on the fly. Interviewers should think about if the role is well established or if the organization is still growing and things just need to be handled when they arise. Finding the balance of structure and creativity will support the role and the person.

Displacing personal feelings on others is difficult for some people to stop. However, overcoming a black and white (right or wrong) personality is difficult for others. Again, what role is the interviewer looking for, and does the individual have a strong mentor who can help the person? More expressive individuals need constant contact of a mentor to refocus them, tell them they're doing well, and to get them back to doing tasks. Black and white individuals need the contact of a manager to walk through situations where hard decisions were made without looking at situations case by case. Roles are generally tailored toward one type. Having too many emotionally expressive employees may drain a manager, so that must also be reviewed so as to not decrease the effectiveness of their future managers.

The way an applicant presents and organizes their thoughts is not an indicator of their ability to complete tasks. It is learning if the person will be rattled by unpredictability and changing of priorities. Some roles lend themselves to predictable deadlines and expectations. For some applicants, that is boring and lacks growth. For others, the predictability shows stability and clarity. Interviewers need to review the role to know if the person will have shifting priorities and if they can handle the fluid nature of the role.

Finally, the way an applicant handles stress is a unique way of learning their eagerness in accomplishing tasks. Is this an individual who is so self-assured in their abilities they will take time and methodically work to a resolution? Do you have the time for them to work through solutions over time in this role? Or is this an individual who is so focused on completing everything that they may look frazzled and appear visually stressed until the task is completed? Does this person interact with the outside public where a stressed demeanor may cause concern?

All people have varying traits in each area and trying to match people with a position is like solving a complicated puzzle. However, when people are placed in the right role, effectiveness is maximized for the person and the organization. The interview situations below are designed to show that people may present themselves in different ways in an interview. Without educating yourself on different personalities and what type of role is available, there is no ability to know based on the information below who is (or who is not) a MOLE individual.

Picture this: You are interviewing for an administrative position in a professional office to support multiple executives and three applicants come in for the interview.

Applicant 1 is quiet. The person tells you they are looking to change industries and speaks positively about their place of employment, through no major elaborations. The applicant is tugging at their sleeves, which you notice because they have tattoos, and there are holes around their mouth, which allows you to know they have a lip ring. The person understands the company from their research online and has brought extra résumés for the room.

Applicant 2 talks more. The person makes you feel like you've known them for years and laughs at your jokes. They arrive in jeans, but that is acceptable for the job they are currently working at. The person recites everything the recruiter told them from memory about the company and tells you an engaging story about how they have worked late hours for the last few years in their hourly role. The person wants a job that has more daytime hours so they can have more of a personal life.

Applicant 3 is the most engaging person of all. They share a very vivid and exciting story to answer every question and is in a professional suit with a designer bag. You get the feeling they were important at their last job and the go-to person. They do not know anything about the organization, but they express that they are a go-getter and willing to learn anything you can throw at them. They are confident they can do the job and have a list of ten references you could call today. Through the interview you find out you have common friends and that their last coworkers were a bit gossipy, but the applicant said they stayed out of it.

A quick review of the scenarios will outline different strengths and weaknesses, but who is the hidden MOLE? First, the company culture should be reviewed. The organization is looking for a person who will be successful in a professional environment, who can report to multiple executives, and who can perform administrative tasks well.

Applicant 1 showed they respect the professional environment by modifying their personal dress (tattoos, piercings) to comply with the professional environment without being told. They have no idea if that is restricted or not. The person performed the pre-hire task of researching an organization and bringing supplies for the group. A manager could assume the person could be assigned a task without excessive direction. The person lacks experience in the organization and was very quiet, leaving minimal room for interpreting answers. Of the three, this applicant was the least engaging, though still nice.

Applicant 2 is extraverted, took control of the interview, and tailored their behavior to those in the room. They had a great memory from the recruiter but did not do additional work to learn. Did they dress for the organization they are attempting to be hired into? The person was able to communicate what they believe their strengths are through working overtime and has a believable story.

Applicant 3 has the most entertaining interview by far, and the stories are stuck in your head. It is almost unbelievable how much this person put up with—no wonder they are leaving their job. They spend most of the interview engaged, relaxed, and storytelling. They sure know about a lot of people at work and in the community. Finally, they clearly placed a lot of focus on their attire to match the environment, wearing a suit and carrying a designer bag to an administrative interview.

After a review of the environment and their behavior, it is still not clear who the MOLE is—if any of the applicants are. Managers should not make decisions on hiring in the moment. It takes time to process what happened in the interview room. Some personalities are overly sensitive, excessively dramatic, and give coworkers (and themselves) permission to underperform. Employers may seek to avoid specific behaviors such as those, but many managers hire exactly what they seek to avoid because interviews are easy for emotionally expressive and extraverted employees to game (whether intentionally or not). Think of it this way, would you rather hire someone who made you laugh in an interview and seemed fun to be around or the person who did their research and hit all the marks on the list?

Depending on who you talk to, the answer may be different. There is a business tip that tells managers to think about if they want to work with that person on weekends or after hours. If so, hire them. If not, don't hire them. We do not generally agree with this recommendation, because hiring a MOLE employee should not be focused on likeability. Also, this tip assumes people will be working at the office on nights and weekends. MOLE employees do not work many nights and weekends in the office. They are efficient, organized, and get their work done. When they work nights and weekends it is typically because they choose to remain in communication with the organization and clients to make lives easier, not because they couldn't get their work done during work hours. Be aware of people who communicate entertaining stories and use those situations to consider how they got themselves into those situations. For example, it sounds positive when a person states they will stay late, but why did they have to stay late in the first place? When seeking a MOLE employee, be on the lookout for persuasive personalities who can talk you in circles, leaving you feeling happy but more confused than when you started. Ask yourself if it makes sense and if you need more clarification.

Required Candidate Screening

Once you think you have determined who the MOLE employee is, the next steps of the interview occur. Commonly required screening for organizations may include background checks, drug screens, candidate testing (such as Microsoft Office or 10-key skill tests), and reference checks. These are done at this stage because the individuals who make it to this point should have the skills to do this job and are true candidates. Now, you have to ensure they can meet the screening requirements.

By standard business practice, organizations should complete employment testing and call former companies or professional references. Be aware any MOLE who is leaving an organization may ask you not to call their current place of employment. Furthermore, their professional references are most likely coworkers. References generally either create unnecessary stress for an applicant or benefit the extraverted applicants who know a lot of people socially. References can easily be falsified. These references will speak highly of them even if they do not know how they are as a worker.

The MOLE Interview

The MOLE interview was created because in the past as we have looked at the performance of the new people we hire into our company, we found if turnover was going to occur, it would happen within the first 12-month period. Virtually all of these were because of a lack of company culture fit. The new hires either do not have the same moral compass we require, the work ethic, or there is something else in their personalities that does not match the behavior of the rest of the staff. To help combat this, we wanted to standardize our interview practices to focus on these skills, and to remove any potential for bias in hiring, including how to handle "gut feelings."

Gut feelings occur when an interviewer cannot quite explain why they like an applicant, but instead have an emotional impression about how the person makes them feel. Gut feelings can result in bias hiring based upon who the interviewer believes and feels comfortable with. Decisions based upon gut feelings do not have any data or facts that support why that person would do well in comparison to other applicants. However, if someone makes an interviewer feel uncomfortable, it is recommended the interviewer try to specifically pinpoint why the individual makes them feel that way. This could be a red flag of a bigger issue.

Today we have experienced success from the development of our new system of interviewing and hiring. We find we are rejecting about thirty percent of the people we would have hired in the past. Our hope is this will improve the number of people we can retain throughout the first year and that these people will be a better overall fit. In the end, we are looking for good people who match our company culture.

The Case of the Midnight Stalker

In my experience in human resources, there have been less than a handful of times that I have felt uncomfortable after an interview. In one such case which we call "the case of the midnight stalker", the person was an active employee up for promotion. We had never received a complaint from any clients with whom he had worked, and his remote supervisor had good feedback and strongly recommended he be promoted.

We had developed the MOLE interview after this person's original hire. As a result, he had never been through the MOLE interview. Since we felt our field supervisor knew him well, and we had not received any complaints - we thought this would be an excellent way to document the benefits of the MOLE interview. The results were quite unexpected. He failed horribly. The MOLE interview did not specifically point out what the problem really was, but it did tell us this person was not right for our company. His evasiveness, the way he answered questions, and at times his outright dishonesty made us halt his promotion. In fact, the interview was so bad, we felt we may need to remove him from the company. There was a lot of confusion and hesitation because the field supervisor liked him because he was willing to work sites for her. She was unable to really tell us much more about him, but his willingness to work was fantastic for her and made her life easier.

It was at that time I made my famous statement, "Aren't we lucky we can remove him in our timeframe?" We thought we had time to continue to review his work, talk to him about the role and continue to see if we had made an error in our interviewing process. When things go wrong, we first must step back and look at ourselves. We started that process thinking we had all the time in the world. This turned out to be a big mistake. Word was getting around we were promoting him and people at the sites realized they might see him more often or work with him more. It all started when one client felt brave enough to call leadership and say they were locking him out and wanted him removed immediately. This was quite confusing for the field supervisor and HR who were in the process of trying to promote him and there were no other complaints. HR handled the complaint just as any other and began to push for specifics. More witness names were listed; more counties were named. This situation started to seem bigger than one issue at one site.

An investigation was launched by human resources, and it turned out he had been stalking many of the female employees and multiple client's employees. There were things similar to going to employee's houses in the middle of the night, taking photographs, and sending text messages to the individuals saying he knew where they lived. As the investigation progressed, we learned no complaints had been previously received because jail officials were afraid of him. We will always be grateful for the individual who spoke up upon hearing his possible promotion plans. The lesson we also learned was to move quickly when it is clear someone needs to be removed.

We ultimately removed him from the company for harassment whereupon he sued us claiming we fired him due to being a male, being heterosexual, and for being African American. His defense rested on "If I were a heterosexual female, or a homosexual male, of a different race, all of this would be okay." That was not true. Six months and many thousands of dollars later, we were successful in defending our position. This case became another example of why you should hire slowly and fire fast. This is not written to say this is the case every time, but during those situations where an interviewer feels uncomfortable, it is wise to attempt to pinpoint what is causing the concern.

We developed our MOLE interview based upon Mark Murphy's book *Hiring for Attitude*. This book suggests hiring for specific values by developing a standard set of behavioral interview questions. The book trains managers to focus on getting a specific example of situations so you can determine what they have done, not hypothetically what they might do in a perfect world. It is the difference of saying, "One day, I saw a patron fall down and performed CPR," versus saying "If anyone would fall down, I think I would perform CPR, though I've never been in that situation." The fact that they've actually done it holds more value.

The questions we have chosen to use from the book and the questions we have created on our own are questions that revolve around upholding our unique culture and ethical expectations. Building your own questions is a process that should be completed with a trusted group of individuals after reading the recommended book *Hiring for Attitude*. This book will walk you through identifying what your company values and expanding off of the main value for question creation. Then, trial and error will allow you to refine your culture and your questions based upon outcomes.

Each interviewer scores the questions on a 1-7 scale. We use a modified scoring system due to aligning it with our evaluations. The 1-7 scale, in our version, holds 5 as a full, solid answer. We liked the answer, the parts were there, but they could have done better. 6's are great answers, and a 7 is rated because we could not ask for anything more. On the other end, a 4 comes in when there are concerns, and it drops all the way down to a 1. An N/A is only scored in the rare situation an applicant says they cannot think of anything and refuses to say anything. In that case, the other answers are reviewed without holding the N/A question against the applicant.

The questions are all set up the same by asking if the person will share a specific example about a task. We ask about a time they didn't know how to do something, and about tasks that failed. Our goal is to hear how they overcame the burden and worked through to a solution. We do not generally recommend more than five questions of this nature to keep the interviews under an hour, and that is typically all that is needed to determine if they are a good fit or not. To reiterate, our questions were formed as a result of reading and interpreting *Hiring for Attitude* for our organization's needs.

The interviewers (no more than five) are all prepared to stay silent, unless asking a question or pushing for more information, though they are trained not to lead the applicant. For example, if an applicant states an issue failed, interviewers would not ask "How was it resolved positively?" because then the applicant will form an answer based on a positive outcome. We are looking for truth, so the question should be phrased more along the lines of, "And then what happened?"

The final question, according to the book, is called the coachability question. It asks a series of layered questions about the individuals' former supervisor. This is not with the intent of learning about the supervisor, but rather determining the type of company culture and supervisor the applicant does or does not prefer to work with or for. Positive comments that support the way things are done in your company is a good sign. Negative comments about their former company culture (such as not liking a boss who doesn't call them daily) may not work if it doesn't match your company culture (of having a traveling manager who only checks in once a week). These are the moments to look at and see if you as a manager can make this person happy. You know the job, they don't.

See the scoring examples below which answered the question, "Could you tell me about a time your task failed?"

Response 1: My son and I planned to make a chocolate molten cake one weekend and, while we followed the instructions, it was a disaster! We decided the cake was not going to beat us. We planned to get the ingredients during the upcoming week and make it again the next weekend. The outcome was much better the second time around and we had delicious cake for dessert.

Score: This answer scored a 6 or 7. Because we already knew the person had the skills to do the job, we were not concerned the answer had nothing to do with her future job. The point was, she told us about her failed problem, how she planned to overcome it, and the positive outcome. She was presented with a failure and problem solved her way through to a solution. These are the individuals we want.

Response 2: Nothing is a true failure. We are in accounting. Everything can be fixed when it is identified and corrected. So I did have a situation where I transposed numbers. My manager found this error when she was comparing reports and the numbers didn't match up. I went back and audited it and found the error. I corrected it and moved forward.

Score: 5. This answer satisfies our question. The honesty of the error, her receptiveness when it was found, and the correction of the error. The score would improve if she had found the error herself, but that is not always within everyone's scope of their role.

Response 3: No. I don't consider anything a failure. They're learning moments. There haven't been any of those I can think of. I really cannot think of a time I have made a mistake.

Score: This would be scored a 3-4. Humans are not perfect and no one believes this person is either. We asked for a specific situation and if the person could not think of one, it would have been preferable to hear that their interview anxiety is not helping them come up with a specific example, but they are sure they have had an error somewhere. They could also let us know that their typical practice is to handle it in a certain way. We don't want perfection. We want honesty and explanation.

At the end of the MOLE interview the applicant is released from the building and the panel stays behind to finish scoring. Then question by question, reviewers share their score and their interpretation of the answer. They share any concerns about the values, the follow through, and/or placing them in the open position. If the decision is made to hire a person, possible tendencies are reviewed with the manager in order to aid in training and transitioning the person to our culture.

Chapter Pearls

- Sourcing gainfully employed people is the ideal way to find employees
- Audit your application and hiring practices to ensure they are appropriate
- Ask specific job-related questions to learn the skillset of applicants
- Keep questions focused on the job; not their personal life
- Conduct required testing/screening consistently
- Use screen-out questions and panel interviewing to ensure a culture fit

| 10 |

Training the MOLE

The two most important things you can do to make your life easier is to hire and adequately train good people. This is often far more complex and takes more work and time than most people understand. The concept of training is about changing people's knowledge and behavior so they are performing at a new level and in ways they never were able to perform before. It requires not only new approaches but behavioral modification, and that is difficult.

It has been said that great leaders see themselves as "chief reminding officers" as much as anything else. Patrick Lencioni's book *The Advantage* suggests you may have to remind your staff as many as seven times before they truly believe, through repetition alone, what you are telling them is true. They may need to hear it from two or three different sources. The problem, according to the book, is leaders confuse the transfer of information to an audience with the audience's ability to understand, internalize, and embrace the message that is being communicated. You as the leader need to be consistent in your communication and in your direction. The final goal of communication is to become fair, firm, and consistent to your direct reports. Using the same stories and examples repeatedly will allow you to become so predictable that when a situation comes up your staff should be able to answer these leadership questions on their own.

In the medical field, almost everyone we train has already learned their craft in medical school or nursing school. They have opinions about how things should be done. This comes from their professors in school, their supervisors at their prior jobs, and possibly a hospital for which they had great respect. They have learned various systems of how to handle things. Some examples include how to pass medications, how to take a history, or how to prescribe medications for a given disease. Your job in training is to take their previous understandings about how things were done, and with new information and behavioral modification, get them to change their behavior so it matches your evidence based established practices.

For example, we do not have a formulary to prevent practitioners from using certain drugs. We believe we can train practitioners to do the right thing. Sometimes this is very problematic, because practitioners will get something in their head they remember and believe, and it is extremely uncomfortable for them to change their behavior. Nurses are no different and will sometimes "see a better way" to do a procedure, which means they will not be following the way they were trained. Generally, they do not understand the reasons behind the seemingly new rules. This can cause chaos in the system.

Training is not telling someone what to do. That has little or no impact on their long-term behavior. A person must understand what they need to do and why they need to do it that way. It is the "why" part that frequently breaks down in training.

Training Timeline

While it is difficult to document a perfect timeline that applies to every job in every industry, the format we have experienced to be most successful is shared in this section. When a person is hired, they have life and work experiences of which you have little knowledge. MOLE leaders do not yet know how the new employee wants to be spoken to, what motivates them to improve, and what demotivates or causes them to freeze. Starting off the employment life with this general structure and applying it to the best of your ability in your organization will help put the framework in for a successful tenure.

When a new person is hired, all orientation work should be completed. Whether that is signing documents, reading training, or traveling to learn skills. Get it scheduled early and get it done. Take the time and do not leave them on their own. Within the first few weeks, they should then be assigned mentors. The mentor program goes on for about three to six months and is discussed in detail in this book. That gives the person outside, but controlled, sources to help them navigate their day-to-day life. From there, they will move into quarterly coaching throughout their employment.

Teaching

Grade schools and high schools are formed around formal didactic lectures with written material to study, weekly tests, and semifinal or final tests at the end of a course. There is some degree of behavioral science behind this system, such as the Ebbinghaus Forgetting Curve. For example, if you listen to a didactic lecture you will forget about 80 percent of what you have been told in about eight days. That is the purpose of the weekly quiz, it forces you to go back and restudy the material at the end of the week. This improves your long-term retention of the material. You need to go back and restudy again in about 30 days. This is the purpose of the midterm and final examinations in high school and college. It forces you to go back review the material to be able to pass a written test. You need to consider these behavioral realities when you are trying to teach your staff a new skill.

For example, if you have a new employee and you are training them on medication pass, they need to review the material again within eight days, and again within 30 days. This really must be done. The supervisor should check that off and remind the employee they need to review the material to ensure they understand it. You must inspect what you expect—a concept we discuss in more detail in Chapter 13.

When it comes to inspecting what you expect, we recommend pre- and post-tests. A pre-test is given to alert the student of the material on which they are going to have to focus. They are not expected to know the answers to the questions, but it will raise questions and focus their mind as they prepare to listen to what is coming in the next few minutes. The post-test, of course, is to see if there is any change in their score or if they have actually learned anything from the lecture you have just given. The post-test should include questions that are the most important parts of the material.

Lectures

There are two basic kinds of lectures. The first type of lecture we are all familiar with is the general educational format to raise your knowledge on a particular subject. For example, in medical school we had lectures on treating arthritis. These included the pathophysiology of arthritis, signs and symptoms, and every medication that could possibly be used to treat it. At the end of the lecture we clearly understood what arthritis was, how it came about, what it looked like, and the range of treatments that could be used to approach it. While these types of lectures are important, they do not provide the tools needed to specifically advise people on how to approach a particular problem. To approach a problem, one has to change behaviors. For a problem such as arthritis, you have to sort through all the signs and symptoms to come to a decision about the diagnosis. Next, you sort through all known treatments and select the best treatment for that disease. This is most likely going to be difficult from the information presented in general lectures. They are not specific enough.

Next is the behavioral modification lecture, here you have to use a very carefully structured format. As a general rule you want to change behavior to solve a problem. The whole system starts with identification of a problem in your company. Something that is not going the way you want it to go. You analyze the problem and break it down to a specific behavior that needs to change to correct the situation. The objective of your lecture is the specific behavior you wish to change. You should not try to change too many behaviors at the same time. Generally, somewhere between two and four behaviors is all you should try to approach. We call these behavioral changes "pearls." We carefully match the objective of the lecture to the pearls that the student is hearing.

For example, we once wanted to reduce the amount of nonsteroidal anti-inflammatory drugs (NSAIDS) such as ibuprofen we were using in our company due to the large number of side effects it was causing. For three years, we lectured on complications and problems in a general educational format. We did not give specific instructions on how to change. After three years we analyzed the number of doses we were giving, and discovered we were prescribing 850,000 doses a year, an enormous amount. It was clear we had to change the format of our lectures. When we changed the format of the lecture to behavioral modification, the first problem was "We are using too many NSAIDS such as ibuprofen and causing too many problems," and the first objective was "Stop using NSAIDS such as ibuprofen." The speech then went on for about eight minutes on the dangers, complications, and problems, ending that very early segment with one pearl, which was "Stop using NSAIDS such as ibuprofen." This was exactly the same wording as the objective. The speech then went to objective number two, and went on for another eight minutes on objective number two, and then gave them the pearl which was exactly the same words as the second objective. At the end of the second brief objective period, we began to build a string of pearls. We repeated the first pearl followed by the new second pearl. We then went to the third objective and repeated the process again, followed by the three pearls given at that time. This allowed the audience to hear the same pearls given over and over again.

When people are sitting in a lecture hall, it is very difficult to maintain their attention to the point they are really focused on what you are talking about and trying to teach. Because of that, if you are using slides, you need to have as many colorful pictures as possible to emphasize the key points you want to make. The brain remembers pictures; it does not remember words. Each small segment should be no more than 6 to 12 minutes long. Most people cannot focus longer than that without an interruption and the restart of a new topic or objective.

Behavioral Modification

People function in a specific way because they believe it is the best way to function. If you get a group of five doctors all sitting around the table talking about how to treat a specific disease, you are probably going to have three or four different versions of how that should be done. Each doctor believes his or her method is the best and the other doctors do not know what they are talking about. This is what causes the confusion. Sometimes it just comes from reading different material and then believing it, other times there is something entirely different going on behind the scenes.

A classic example of a behavioral modification problem was getting doctors to wash their hands in-between patients many years ago. Everyone knows this is a good idea, and doctors understand the whole concept of microbiology and infectious disease. They know how disease is spread from one patient to another. Yet, they were not washing their hands. In the past, this has been a problem in virtually all hospitals. The question was why? People had been trained and people know the science behind it. Why was it not happening?

It turns out when the doctors were interviewed in depth, there were many reasons they did not like to wash their hands. One, it takes upwards to sixty seconds from the time you start until you finish and dry your hands. When we originally started to practice medicine, it was not uncommon to see 50 or 60 patients in the course of one full day of work. If you have to wash your hands between each one and it takes a minute, you have lost an hour of working time. An hour of working time for a doctor might be seeing at least five patients. If the doctor earns $60 per patient, that amounts to $300 the doctor has lost washing his hands. In addition, other doctors said washing your hands often takes all of the oil out of your skin, and you can't reapply lotion every time because then you feel greasy when you see the next patient. Consequently, their skin breaks down and they get rashes and cracks around their fingernails. Everyone agreed based upon the lost income and the breakdown of the skin on the hands that washing your hands did not seem like a good idea for doctors. This identification of a pain point leads us to the concept of earthworms.

Earthworms

Earthworms react entirely based upon pain and pleasure. Of the two, pain is the most important. People are no different. In the example above regarding doctors washing their hands, you can see they believed the pain of washing their hands with the skin breakdown and lost income was far more real than the pleasure of seeing reduced illnesses in patients later.

You see, when you run into resistance, there is probably something behind the resistance you may not be aware of or understand. It is going to be critical for you to try to sort that out if you have a particular problem with an individual.

A solution to the resistance problem is to create more pain in not doing the behavior you want than in doing it. For example, in the case of doctors washing their hands, a concerted program had to be set up so doctors were literally monitored as they made rounds in the hospital by nurses on every floor. Any failure to wash hands between patients was reported to the head of the department of medicine, which is followed by an embarrassing discussion of the problem. Once the concept of pain was established, the problem was very quickly resolved and it became a pattern and habit, no longer needed close monitoring. Today technology has developed alcohol wipes and hand gels that can be used in front of the patient with no time lost.

Remember whenever you run into resistance in trying to change someone's behavior, always think of the earthworm and of the pain and the pleasure. Try to figure out where the resistance is coming from.

Training Tourists

Another problem you will run into when you are in the process of training, usually with a group, are training tourists. They are there to be entertained, but they have not come to be trained. They may appear to be attentive, but their minds are somewhere else. There is no place for training tourists in your lectures and your training seminars. Always be on the watch for this, and if you think you have got someone who is not paying attention, focus on them and ask them specific questions so you can get them engaged in your lecture.

Visceral Training

As we looked at how to modify people's behaviors, it became very clear the times we had our behavior modified was when we were upset about something. While it is generally taught you should not correct a person in front of a group, there are times when it is necessary to make a point to the individual and the group. The issue is bigger than a single individual. An example is being deposed in a lawsuit over something difficult. We believe we can create teaching methods that contain visceral impact or "visceral training". In this particular case, Dr. Johnson recalls the following story:

A patient had gone to the emergency room and was told by the emergency room physician after doing an X-ray, she needed to increase fluids and was given some decongestants. She came to my office to follow up. She said she didn't feel much better. I reviewed the chest X-ray, which had been read by the radiologist and his diagnosis was completely different from the ER physicians—it showed congestive heart failure, or too much fluid. Rather than pushing fluids, she should have been reducing fluids. I discussed this with her, recommended she go to the hospital, but I did not really emphasize it. She said she didn't think she felt that bad and preferred not to go to the hospital. Consequently, I gave her medication and sent her home. Unfortunately, she had an irregular heart rhythm that night and passed away. A lawsuit followed and I was deposed. In the lawsuit everyone agreed I recommended she be admitted to the hospital, but the problem was I had not emphasized it adequately. In retrospect, I could not disagree. From that point on my behavior was changed, and forevermore when

I made a recommendation, patients always understood what I thought was important or needed to be done, and I documented this well.

One of the new models we have started to use is deposing people using their own paperwork. This can be paperwork from human resources, progress notes, or any other type of instrument you want to use that has been incorrectly filled out, poorly filled out, or makes no sense at all. For this to really work it has to be done in front of people. The truth is people always say, "Never correct or discipline someone in front of other people," and we agree with that to a point. However, if you want to change somebody's behavior, focus on a thing they themselves have to agree is bad behavior, and walk through how to correct it in front of everyone.

Scorecards and Scoreboards

Two of the key instruments used in visceral training are called scorecards and scoreboards. For a long time, we had trouble trying to get complete continuous quality improvement (CQI) reports. A CQI is a meeting to discuss continuing quality improvement in a particular project. They are held periodically, usually every three to four months, and they discuss all of the problems that have been addressed since the prior meeting. There is also a large number of statistics that are reported during these meetings. The lack of statistics we were seeing was quite dismal. The first time we began to look at this we were down to 20-25 percent completeness rate. Of those that were complete, the majority of them were not done in a timely manner, not within the 30-day period from the time they were conducted. In addition, many of the numbers that were put in made no sense at all and a simple glance at them told you that they were wrong, and yet they were submitted as part of the permanent record with incorrect numbers. At other times, the action items at the beginning of the report that were not complete were not moved to the action items at the end, which were assigned to the next CQI period. There were many things wrong with these, and there were very few that were accurate or complete.

We lectured on the subject, showed examples, worked with individuals, and over a period of the next year and half to two years, we made no progress at all. Then one day we wrote down each individual score of the people responsible for the reports on a piece of paper, which is the same as a scorecard (like a grade school report card) and gave it to the individuals. Most of the employees found the report cards interesting, but they had no context to determine if they were going good work or substandard work. Then we built a scoreboard, which showed all of the individuals with their names and their scores, and everybody could look at it. Of course, we had one or two that were excellent, and all the rest were failing one way or another. The response was dramatic—most people just refused to believe it was even true. They did not believe they were as bad as they were. What we noticed within the next four-month period was a marked improvement. It was not good enough, but there was clear improvement. Gradually over a period of about a year, the scores improved to the point we had 80 percent compliance across the board. The next year we moved up to 85 percent. Then it went up to 90 percent compliance.

Scoreboards compare people or teams against one another. Think of a high school football game. At any time, you can look at the scoreboard and see what quarter you are playing in and who is ahead at a glance. That is the key point of scoreboards. Your staff can look at a scoreboard and see what their personal score is relative to their peers. This is a visceral method of training people to improve performance. You can come up with a scoreboard for almost anything. Think about it. Look at the problem and see how you could use a scoreboard in your training to improve the performance of the people under you.

Scoreboards are a powerful way to demonstrate to people when they are or are not executing. It all comes down to the data you are scoreboarding. Earlier we mentioned statistics can be kept to see if people are completing their action items in the assigned time frame. This could be put on a scoreboard where all individuals can see where they fall on their execution compared with their coworkers. This removes any debate whether they are completing their action items as directed and it helps to numerically define their ability to execute. For example, 63 percent of the time over the last month you completed all of your action items. That means, that over one-third of the time I cannot rely on you to get the action items completed as assigned. Then you can start a conversation with that individual to help them execute at a higher level. Always consider scoreboards when you want to break through resistance and improve people's performance.

Scorecards are done privately; this is more like your school report card. It should include a specific list of job descriptions and how you are doing. Again, we rank these on a scale of 1 to 7. A 4 on the scale means individuals are doing their job exactly as they are told. Nothing more, nothing less. A 5 is where we endeavor employees to live. Spotting opportunities and doing well, consistently. A 6 or a 7 comes when employees do big things and swing up for a specific reason. They typically come back down to a 5 or 6 later, once they get back into their regular routine. A 4 is behavior that is being tolerated but not appreciated, and 3 or less requiring specific action items to improve.

Scorecards are discussed privately with the individual during our quarterly coaching meetings. If a person receives a 1 or a 2, you should seriously consider why this person is with your organization.

Dr. Johnson recalls the following story:

Years ago, I was the doctor at a project in Wisconsin. I would read all of the nurses' progress reports, and a good share of them were missing data or made no sense as I read down the flow of the chart. I created a game called "What is wrong with this progress note?" At the end of the day, I would gather all of the nurses around and would pick up one of the incomplete progress notes. I would put that in front of everyone and ask all of the nurses to look at it and identify what was wrong with the note. The nurse that had written the note was initially embarrassed and not happy about this system. All of the nurses who had not written the note were very engaged and would aggressively look to find the errors. It may have been as simple as a missing date or a signature line that had been neglected. The problem was identified quickly.

The first time I did this, about 30 percent or more of the notes were not adequately filled out. By the next week, it was probably no more than 10-15 percent that were inadequate. By the fourth week, every note was perfect. From that point on the notes stayed perfect for the additional two years I was there. In fact, the nurses were so convinced if something were wrong with one of their notes I would find it, so they trained themselves to get into a pattern of always doing things correctly and we never again had a problem. A year after I left that project, I returned to do some training. I reviewed a few progress notes and they were still perfect. A couple of years later I came back again, and by that time there had been staff turnover and I began to notice some lapses again because there had not been adequate training or follow up. The point of the story is this: you can find a visceral training method for anything you need to train. You just have to sit down, think about it, and figure out the proper venue to do it. It is clear people do not like to have their errors and mistakes pointed out to other people. There is no more powerful instrument in changing behavior than a properly conducted visceral training. Properly done, it can even become a game and fun for everyone. Over the course of the few weeks I conducted the game, "What is wrong with this progress note," the staff really got into it and were deeply engaged. They wanted to find everyone else's mistakes. Consider visceral training for your more difficult training modules.

Concept Penetration

At our company we carefully poll the audience to grade our lecturers on their style, material, and relevance of topic to get an overall view of how an individual is presenting. Patterns begin to form of who our best lecturers are, and who needs more help and advice in constructing their programs.

After one of the lectures was delivered by our highest-rated speaker, we passed out a small questionnaire and simply asked the audience to write down the three or four key topics the author was trying to convey. The results were startling. There was no consistency or understanding of what the key points were, and there were no modifications or changes in anybody's behavior going forward. This forced us to really focus on lectures that are modifying behavior; trying to change a maximum of four pieces of behavior and driving home the points again and again using clear objectives followed by clear pearls of behavioral change. At the end of the lectures we ask the audience to write down precisely what behavioral changes the lecturer was advising, the results now indicate we are running in the 70-90 percent understanding of the key points. This seems to indicate to us that because of the way we are structuring these lectures we are getting a much higher concept penetration, an understanding which will then lead to changes in behavior.

It's interesting to note as we looked at the percent of penetration of each of our concepts, from one down to three or four, the penetration percentage drops. It may start at 80 percent for concept one, 70 percent at two, 55 percent at three, and all the way down to 40 percent penetration for number four. When you give a lecture or behavioral modification training that has three or four basic concepts, you must be aware the longer you talk, the less impact you are going to have, and the less the audience will remember. Because of this, innovative ways of engaging the audience must be used. These may include question and answers, short videos, or animated sequences in your presentations. If these concepts do not sink in, it is a waste of time for everyone.

There are three basic phases to the development of a lecture. In phase one, you identify a problem area. Something you wish to stand up in front of a group and present that will change their behavior in a way to improve overall productivity. In phase two you determine the exact behavior you want to see changed. Finally, you begin to look for any measurable data in phase three to see if you have made any changes after the talk.

For example, after lecturing for three years and raising awareness of the side effects of non-steroidal drugs, our company was still using over 850,000 doses a year. We wanted to see usage reduced and to see the numbers come down. In phase two of the development of a lecture you design the talk ensuring the objectives match the pearls and ensure there are not too many objectives to try to achieve in the lecture. When you are standing in front of a group, most people cannot focus for more than approximately eight seconds before their mind starts to wander or they start to pick up on a distraction in the room. Because of that, the lecturer must be taught to move, be active, and change their tone of voice. In other words, perform while on stage lecturing. The slides mentioned earlier need to be colorful with pictures and to the point. There cannot be a lot of words that the presenter reads to the audience. After the lecture is delivered, we need to look carefully at the feedback received on the presentation, the concept penetration, and the overall effect of the lecture. If there are some concepts that did not have good penetration, we would need to go back and review that section of the lecture and make alterations prior to the next time the material is presented. For example, if concepts one and two were in the 70-90 percent penetration range but concept three was in the 35 percent range, we would review concept three in the presentation.

Phase three involves looking at the data 6-18 months from now to determine whether permanent behavioral changes have been made. In the case of non-steroidal drugs, we dropped our doses from 850,000 to below 300,000. The documented side effects dropped markedly. Over the next year, our doses dropped to less than 150,000, and side effects continued to drop drastically.

Writing a behavioral modification lecture is far more complicated than writing a general information lecture. You have to put a lot more thought into it and have very clear goals. You need to look for metrics before you give the lectures and monitor again months down the road, so you can see if you actually changed behavior. In the end, if you follow these guidelines your training will become very powerful and you will be able to make permanent changes in how your company functions.

The Slack in the Screw

In teaching and training it is not uncommon to believe there are certain things that are so intuitive you do not need to teach them. An example is training doctors to wash their hands in-between patients. While you would think this would be intuitive, to some people it is not, and you need to monitor them to ensure it is done. The biggest problem with people who are experts in their field and who have a responsibility for training is there are some things that are so intuitive to them because they have done them for so many years they have forgotten there was once a time they didn't know them. We like to call this issue "the slack in the screw."

Dr. Johnson recalls the following story:

Many years ago before I became a physician, I was a tool and die maker working in a factory. One day we hired a young man who was new to the job and was not a trained machinist. It was my job to train him on the use of a milling machine. This is a large machine with a cutting wheel that shaves pieces of steel off as the table is cranked across the cutting tool. I demonstrated how to clamp the piece down, how to put the cutting wheel in place, and what speed to run it at. I made sure he had on his safety apron and glasses, and he stood on the correct side of the table. Then I said, "Do you think you have it?" He said, "Absolutely, I've got it." I turned around and began to walk away, and he turned the machine on to start milling on this piece of steel. Almost immediately there was a loud crack and a bang, and pieces of steel were flying all over the department. It was a miracle no one was injured or killed. I ran back over as quickly as I could and said, "What happened?" He said, "I don't know, I did it just like you showed me." I said, "Show me again what you did." He went through the motions again, and as he began to crank the table toward the cutting wheel I said, "Oh, you didn't take the slack in the screw out." He looked at me like I was from Mars. He had no idea what the slack in the screw was.

Every threaded bolt has a little looseness between the bolt and the nut that fits onto it. If you screw a light bulb into a threaded socket, it will have a little looseness that you can shake up and down. This looseness is the slack. When you are dealing with a precision cutting machine such as a milling machine, you have to be sure you are pushing against the slack so the table doesn't jerk if the tool grabs the steel and pulls it quickly away from you. The next tooth will take a much larger bit and break. He hadn't thought of this. This was so intuitive to me because I'd been doing it for ten years, it didn't occur to me that I would have to explain it to somebody else. When working at a machine shop, one is always concerned about the slack in the screw, but when I talk to the people I work with today, there isn't a single person who understands what I'm talking about. When you are explaining the details of a procedure, make sure you have not left out some key point you know because of your experience, but that no one would understand without the same level of experience. Make sure you are training down to every little detail you can think of. When something happens that "should've been intuitive," remember the slack in the screw. This was my fault, not his.

MAC Programs

Occasionally you are going to have a problem that is so serious you have to change an entire system. Writing a good, clear, and complete progress note was one of those problems we had to address. The doctors were the worst. They absolutely did not document adequately. The nurses frequently did not have the proper flow of information from the time of the complaint to the objective date to the assessment and the plan. It became critical we not only train people in how to do this, but that we create what we call a MAC. A MAC is a "memory" prompt followed by "action," followed by almost immediate "consequences."

The work Dr. Johnson did at the project in Wisconsin discussed in the visceral training section was really a MAC. They had the memory prompt (pre-printed progress note) that had to be filled out a specific way, followed by the action they took, followed by the consequences of having him sit there and point out their failings. In the sites where a doctor is coming in and filling in a progress note, the nurse should review it as soon as they are done. The immediate consequences should be to put that right back under their elbow and have them complete it if they failed to include any important information. Some examples include not listing the duration of illness, any teaching they gave to the patient, or a note about the next follow up (even if it is just "as needed"). All of this should be recorded.

MAC programs are specific programs to handle a specific problem. Another example of a MAC program is a problem Dr. Johnson had when he was in practice:

We would get about one-half to three-quarters of an inch of laboratory reports that came in every day. Every doctor had to look at their reports and sign them. What I saw was doctors just signing the corner without really looking at the laboratory data. Occasionally important information was missed. We instituted a MAC program, which required the doctor to circle the most abnormal lab, even if it was still within the normal range. That meant the doctor had to actually look at the reports and think about the abnormalities. You could tell by whether or not a lab was circled as well as signed if that doctor had actually looked at the numbers, if they did not it was immediately put back under his elbow so that he had to review it again. There was a consequence to not following through. These are MAC programs, and as you run into various problems, see if you can devise a MAC program to help with training and behavioral modification. If you have trouble designing these, talk to your supervisors and the people to you report to and see if they can assist you.

Consistency in Training

A company such as ours is at high risk to have different qualities and consistency of training. Because of this, we believe you need to have the same training materials across the board. If possible, you need to have videos to play while instructors are sitting there to answer questions. These will be consistent across all of your regions; you need to keep records on who and what you have trained.

In the past we have recorded many of our training sessions on DVDs. The benefit is it is the same material and the same lecture, which gives consistency in training. Once again, it's important to have the instructor sitting in on the training sessions to answer questions or to point out any misunderstandings the audience may have.

The problem with DVDs is they became dated very quickly. We had to solve that problem with a learning management system (LMS). This will allow us to present the same trainings, always trying to keep in our 8 to 12 minute range with one behavioral modification or one key point we are making per lecture. Then, if in a year or two that information begins to change or becomes obsolete, we can quickly redo the video and put it in the LMS. LMS is online and can be accessed 24/7. This will constantly keep our staff up to date and make annual training much easier and more valuable.

Chapter Pearls

- Understand your onboarding timeline
- Teach and guide through training and lectures
- Inspect what you expect through follow up
- Find where resistance comes from (earthworms)
- Engage tourists
- Use visceral (emotional) training
- Use scorecards and scoreboards
- Track concept penetration
- Train every step; every detail (slack in the screw)
- Develop MAC programs
- Train consistently

| 11 |

Mentoring for the MOLE

Training and educating a new employee takes a lot more work and time than most people believe. It goes far beyond teaching the person the necessary job skills. This is where mentoring the employee comes into play. Mentoring is an ongoing process that can last three to six months depending upon the position and the complexity of the information that needs to be learned. It is conducted not by just one person, but an entire team of people who each know their particular responsibility when it comes to mentoring.

To begin the process, the employee's supervisor will need to spend time demonstrating the necessary job skills. This should be done slowly and clearly, demonstrating the correct procedures and where the supervisor has observed errors made in the past. This will ensure the errors will not be duplicated by your new employee. When the supervisor is convinced they have trained them adequately in all of the job skills, we have to remember a good percentage of the material presented to the employee will be forgotten in the next eight days. Because of that, the supervisor needs to continue mentoring the person by working with them daily or every other day for the next week or two to ensure things are going correctly and the employee understood the necessary job skills and is performing properly. It is the follow up portion that is the mentoring. This needs to go on as long as necessary for the supervisor to be confident things are going well. The employee will have their first coaching session, which is an evaluation of their function, in 30 days. The mentoring from the supervisor will need to go on in some fashion for at least three to six months.

Another mentor should be someone of the same level so they would have a similar mindset of the responsibilities of the role. The job of a coworker is to teach and mentor them on the culture of the company to help them get along with the clients and staff with whom they will be working. Over time, they should come to understand all the nuances of working in a new environment. This person of the same level may have the same job title but have been on the job for a longer period and could provide tips and tricks to effectively learn and operate the role.

The other two or three individuals in a mentorship program should be assigned with very specific tasks to inspire and encourage the new hire. For example, this can be a human resources person assigned to a role that is more at risk for breaking policies or dealing with employee behavior. The mentor would not focus on the black and white rules and education, instead, the mentor would use the opportunity to ask the new hire how they are doing in their new supervisory role or what challenges they have faced taking care of patients who may have formerly been high school acquaintances, for example. The mentor learns the individual's feeling on situations, and has enough knowledge to be able to suggest a course of action if the individual needs any help. The mentor tries to "pave the way" for new hires by using their established business relationships and company structure understandings.

Finally, we are finding great success in having someone from the company mentor the person from the standpoint of personality testing to help them understand their personality and those with whom they will be working. The important thing to understand is how various personalities interact with one another and how they get along. This is an area if a new employee can understand and learn, it will make their lives much easier.

In today's world, information technology is critical. Every new employee has new programs and shortcuts to getting information to learn.

It is critical the IT department has someone who mentors on a regular basis to assist the new employee with any areas of difficulty and try to smooth the way going forward.

The next area to consider for a mentor is someone from the training division. If this employee is in a senior position or in a position where they will be training other people, they are going to need ongoing advice in how to instruct and deliver training sessions. As we have mentioned earlier, training is not simply telling someone what to do. It is an ongoing process in which the trainer is responsible for ensuring the trainee clearly understands the material and has the right behavioral modification to perform a new job or process.

The next area to consider is communications training. There are few areas in business that waste more time and money than poor communication. This includes under communication and overcommunication. Please refer to our chapter on communication for a more detailed discussion of this area. Communication from the new employee needs to be monitored and any areas of improvement need to be communicated on a regular basis. Properly done this will improve communication, reduce waste, and make everyone's life easier.

Mentors should contact their mentee weekly for the first few weeks until their conversations become more natural. Once established, regular meetings may not need to be scheduled if the communication is flowing between mentors and the mentee is performing well. The process becomes more customized by the individual.

To be direct, orientation is a process that ends. Training never, ever, ends. Training is ongoing at companies. So, while the initial data dump of information will end and the mentorship continues, the employee will need to be evaluated at about 30 days. This is one of the forced interactions to occur to allow the employee to bring up anything they want to regarding their new life at this organization. It is not a place for surprising employees with negative feedback or for embarrassment. Throughout the employment relationship, issues should be brought up early and often for resolution. The 30 day review is the time to document what has occurred and how the employee has moved past it successfully or unsuccessfully (with correction plans).

Mentorship continues and the employee then reaches 90 days. Again, their employment life is reviewed, performance status and issues are discussed, and things are tweaked as needed. This is further instilling the type of company they are in and the type of leader you are. Phasing out of the 90 day evaluation, the mentorship relationships will start to slow and may change. Some relationships will remain because of the secure bonds and assistance they have received, others will become more ad hoc mentorship for specific, intermittent issues. That is to be expected. By this point, the employee should have a grasp of how to behave and perform well.

While it depends on hire date, within the first year of employment the employee may undergo a 360 evaluation of their reputation with the organization alongside every other employee. Once feedback is received, employees look at the outcomes as they relate to behaviors and value. This is what others think of them—their reputation. This rarely has to do with their day-to-day job tasks, but it could. An open discussion must be held by the MOLE leader to ensure the employee identifies themes and areas of improvement and does not spend excessive or unproductive time trying to figure out who said what or justify motives. The goal is to improve. Some annoyances do not need to be improved upon, but there is probably a grain of truth in any of the feedback. 360s can be emotional, but they can also be very rewarding to see positive feedback from peers.

Once through the mentorship cycle and evaluations, employees will enter quarterly coaching sessions with managers. These are every three to four months and are manager-led. When these concepts are new to an organization it may be useful to use a third-party mentorship coach or third-party mentorship/coaching organization to further assist the manager in guiding these interactions in an unbiased and informative way. Third-party coaches or third-party organizations benefit companies in order to allow for an unbiased opinion regarding the employee's performance and goals. Using a third-party mentorship/

coaching organization helps by providing tips, examples, and other resources for managers and employees to use in order to communicate effectively and efficiently. Coaches also can bring up issues or uncomfortable items on behalf of the manager or employee to get the information discussed with a mediator. It also allows for unbiased processes, consistent support, and a standardized process for managers and employees to follow. The third-party coaches or organizations are there to ensure the overall vision is met and there is continuous improvement by identifying action items, maintaining a productive experience, and avoiding depreciating one-way conversations.

An example of the benefit of a coach occurred when a manager met with an employee who shared she was going to end up quitting due to having a child. The manager proceeded to document and share she needed to replace the person in the fall because she was pregnant. The coach redirected the manager and the employee back to the issue, which was not the employee was pregnant. The coach reinforced the employee's goal to resign her role and the great business relationship the employee and manager had that resulted in the employee sharing this goal so early. From there, a transition plan was discussed to help the employee to transition out when they were ready. The employee was kept involved in the replacement of her position, and even had an opportunity to train the new person.

Employees share what they feel is going well or what they feel they need assistance on. They update the MOLE leader on their goals and what they like about the organization. They update the MOLE leader on what they dislike about the organization and what they are having challenges with as well. Again, these are structured, forced interactions so MOLE leaders and employees do not get lost in the day-to-day whirlwind and forget to take the time. Goals and action items are updated and sent back out for documentation purposes. This process is defined in detail in the next chapter, Coaching and the MOLE.

The Cadence of Contacts

At the beginning of this chapter, we said mentoring needs to go on for three to six months depending on the complexity of the job and of the information needed to be imparted. To begin, each one of the mentors needs to determine the frequency they need to reach out and communicate with a new employee. For the supervisor this may be daily to start. For IT or HR, it may be no more than weekly depending upon the judgment of the mentor. Coworkers need to stay in communication daily initially to reassure the new employee they have a friend in the company who is there to support them. Other mentors such as people mentoring communication may reach out no more than once a week. These contacts typically would be brief—three to five minutes—and in person if possible. This is not something that should be attempted via email or text. It is critical the new employee has personal contact with the people who are there to help them.

Examples of mentoring phone calls could be if a coworker mentor knows a new employee is going into a meeting with a client. The mentor places a call to the employee to assist in handling the situation. *"Hello John, this is Mary, I understand you are going to be meeting with Administrator Bill today. I have known Bill for some time, and he is a good person, and is fair. He does not like to chitchat and wants to get right down to business to make his meetings short and to the point. In the past, I have seen him get upset with people if they got too chatty. Also, he completely lost faith in someone when he asked them a question and they guessed the answer, giving incorrect information. They were unable to work together going forward. If he asks you a pointed question you don't know, tell him you're not sure and will find out. Make sure to follow up quickly with him. Call me after the meeting. I'm interested in how it goes. Talk to you later. Goodbye."*

Another example may be: *"Hello John, this is Harry, I am part of your mentoring team working on communication, and I noticed you are doing a good job. Your communications are accurate and to the point. The only area I could help you with is to consider the number of people you are adding on* to your email chain. Many times, I suspect they don't need this information. It is a judgment call and I understand you want people to know what you're doing. The truth is, if there are too many copies of email going to people that do not have actionable items, they will tend to get confused and waste time trying to figure out if they should be doing something. This is just something to consider going forward. Overall, you're doing a good job. Call me if you have any questions. Talk to you later."

Once again, these contacts should be no more than three to five minutes, unless the employee clearly needs to talk at great length about a problem they are having.

The job of the mentor is really to coach the new employee in their particular area(s). The first formal coaching session should be with the supervisor and will come at the end of the first 30 days. Out of that, a written report should come that analyzes how the new employee is doing with job skills, communication, and any observations the supervisor has regarding the employee fitting into the organization's culture. The 30-day coaching session should be face-to-face, lasting from 60-90 minutes. It should include probing questions, and some examples include:

- Is the job what they expected it to be?
- What are the most difficult portions of the job?
- Is there any advice they would have for us on changes in the company that could make things easier for everyone?
- Is the amount of paperwork appropriate?
- Are they getting the right amount of support from their mentoring team?

At the end of this session, a lengthy report is entered and given to the employee with new action items and ways to continue to improve.

The next formal coaching session takes place at the end of 90 days. Again, the same basic material is reviewed. Always look for areas we call "shoves." These are things that could literally cause the employee to leave the company. You need to look for them and be aware of them on an ongoing basis, so you can either correct them or decide if possibly you hired the wrong individual.

Once you've gone through the first 90 days with this new employee and are convinced the mentoring is going well, you will transition to three-month coaching sessions. At the 30- and 90-day coaching sessions it is important you communicate with all of the mentors to get their feedback about how the new employee is doing, and any strengths or weaknesses they have perceived.

Properly performed mentoring is one of the most important things you can do to reduce turnover and ensure proper training in your company.

Chapter Pearls

- Mentoring takes a team
- Orientation ends; training never ends
- Cadence of contacts is critical

| 12 |

Coaching for the MOLE

Once you get past the first 90 days, a routine series of meetings every three to four months is set up for in-person coaching. At some point, the employee will no longer need all of the mentors. It will come down to simple meetings between the employee and the supervisor. These coaching meetings will last about 90 minutes and are very structured. Annual reviews are no longer done to determine strengths, weaknesses, or pay rates. We recommend coaching.

Coaching Review Philosophy

The overall purpose of coaching reviews is to make your staff better in order to make your life easier. Coaching reviews are not an exercise to catch them in an error or do a "gotcha" review. The entire focus of the review should be these are good people and their jobs should be secure, but they are not perfect. Therefore, you can assist them to get even better than they are. It is not uncommon to begin the coaching by asking the question, "Are you perfect?" Of course, no one can say they are perfect, so the next question is, "Why not? What are you working on? Is there anything I can help you work on so together we can make you stronger?" Sometimes the employee will hit upon the main point you wish to coach on, and sometimes they don't. If they don't then you continue to have a conversation with them until you can lead them into those areas you believe they do need to focus on to improve. Coaching reviews should be completed at least four times per year with full time or part time staff.

Coaching of MOLE leaders is far more in-depth than mentoring. We recommend you set aside at least an hour and a half every three months to do an in-depth analysis of the competence and performance of leaders. We generally start with a 20 or 30 minute general discussion of how things are going in their departments and what problems or difficulties they may be having with their staff and direct reports. We ask them to bring MOLE scores and scorecards on all of their staff, so we can see which employees are causing them the most problems and which are the most supportive. We then discuss their plans for assisting the weakest employees to make them stronger or replace them.

CAMPS-T

Following a 20 or 30 minute general discussion, we go into an extensive study of their CAMPS-T report. This acronym is derived from Competency, Awards, Meaningful, Professional Progress, Shoves, and Tugs. The CAMPS-T tells us what the employee believes is most important, most meaningful, and guides us on any further training or assistance we can give them to accelerate in their position.

It starts out with a general discussion of the "new competencies" the employee demonstrated over the last three month period. This may be a new computer program they have learned to use or may have been a new technique they have developed for dealing with difficult employees. It is always a new competence of which the employee is proud.

The next part is the "new competencies" the leader believes will be necessary to learn over the next three-month period. This may be new skills they are going to need going forward relative to a new client, a contract, or some other interpersonal skill of which they believe they could benefit. If the company can help them with courses or training this certainly should be supplied at that time.

After competence, we discuss the "awards" the leader has received. This may be thank-you notes, certificates, of the year awards, educational milestones, or any other of a long list of awards and recognition the leader has been awarded. Following that we ask how many "awards" and thank you's the leader has given to their employees and people who have assisted them. We always expect MOLE leaders will give more recognition and awards than they are receiving themselves.

The next area we look at is "meaningful accomplishments" over the last three months. This will tell you what kinds of things the employee feels good about. What makes them feel they have accomplished something important and meaningful to them. It may be a particular project they were able to complete on time and under budget. It may be a new person they have hired or were able to train to a higher level. Whatever these meaningful things are, it is very important for you to review this in detail with them because this tells you what motivates and drives them. The next question is what "meaningful things" they expect to accomplish in the next three months. Again, this allows you to look forward to those things that cause real excitement in your employee and to keep them focused on the things they enjoy doing.

The next area is "professional progress." What new professional progress did they demonstrate in the last three months relating to their role at work or personally? Maybe they are enrolled in a certificate program. Maybe they attended a certain conference to obtain a skill or maybe they are going to attend an online webinar. After this the question is what "new professional progress" do they expect to demonstrate in the next three months? Again, this will help you focus your staff member on those things that demonstrate their personal growth and areas you may assist them in improving.

"Shoves" is the next area. These are critically important. A shove is anything that over a period of time would tend to push or shove the employee out of the company. What are the negatives this employee has to run into on a daily basis that are difficult to handle? Are they thrown into a mix of employees that simply are not functioning well and they find it difficult on a daily basis to get along with them? Are they dealing with equipment that is old and outdated and doesn't function at the level it should? The area of shoves is one of the most critical areas of the entire evaluation. Employees are frequently not open to talking about shoves, but you need to gently work with them and probe them until you can try to get at anything that is a negative for them. This is your one chance to see if there is anything you can do to assist them in making it better.

"Tugs" is the final area. Tugs are things that make you feel good about the company, things the employee enjoys. It may have been an award they won, and they felt really good about the whole thing. There may have been a new employee they were able to identify, hire, and bring into the company that has been performing well.

Overall, the CAMPS-T evaluation is one of the most important areas of the entire quarterly coaching review because it allows you to dig into the personality of your MOLE employee, what motivates them, what demotivates them, what professional progress they have grown over the last year and how many new competencies they have developed. By the time you go through four of these reports over the period of a year you will see serious growth in your employee. These may be areas the employee has grown but you have forgotten about, and are very important when you are looking at the percent of raise for this person. Remember, the person who trains themself and is more competent is worth more money to the company and therefore should receive a higher raise. CAMPS-T evaluation will show you how your MOLE employees will blossom under your guidance.

MOLE Test

The next area we review is the MOLE test. After we developed the concept of the MOLE employee, we struggled with how to define and measure a MOLE employee so their skillset could be compared against other employees. For weeks we were trying to come up with a solution to the problem. One night Dr. Johnson woke up at 2:00 a.m. and the entire MOLE test was in his head. He began to write as quickly as he could before he forgot what the specific questions were. By the time he finished he had completed seven specific questions that allowed us to measure a person's ability to be a MOLE and allowed us to compare their MOLE scores with other employees.

The MOLE test is a form containing seven questions you as the leader fill out concerning each of your direct reports. This will help you to quantify who is making your life easier and who is making it more difficult. When you put all of your employees on a scoreboard you can quickly see who you need to spend the most time with and who is making your life easier.

The first statement is, "The employee never causes a problem I have to solve." This addresses the issue of employees who create trouble and make you stop what you are doing to resolve it. It may be they have upset a client and now you're the one who has to calm everyone down and get it back on track. Maybe they got into an argument with another employee, and now you have two people who don't want to work together. This statement addresses difficult employees and helps you identify the causes of lost time just trying to straighten problems out. This does not evaluate when your employees actually need help and they bring problems you work through together.

Statement two is, "The employee calls with recommendations to solve issues before they become problems." A MOLE employee constantly looks ahead and predicts what is coming at them. If we can solve these problems before they reach a critical state, life is much easier. In order to accurately evaluate this, you will need to keep records and notes on how the employee is functioning when they bring problems to you with solutions. This will help you to understand if they do have the ability to make these recommendations before the problems have developed.

The next section is the 360 performance evaluation ranking compared to other people in the company. We put all of the employees who get 360s on one big spreadsheet and divide them into sevenths. You are then given a numerical value for the group you are in with 7 being the best and 1 being the worst.

"Rank the employee's overall performance in accomplishing goals" is the next statement. As we go down through the individual's personal goals, we will be able to see how many of them are performing and how many are not getting done.

"The employee has complete autonomy in decision-making" is statement five. There are employees that for whatever reason simply cannot make a decision. They don't want to take responsibility, and every time a decision has to be made, they bring it to you and keep bouncing things back and forth until you end up giving them the answer. That is not a MOLE employee. We want people who can make good decisions. It's okay if they make a decision, bring it to you, and tell you what they've decided for your approval. We don't want a situation where the employee is coming to you to "dump monkeys on your back".

The next statement is "The employee surrounds themselves with competent people." We have had many leaders over the years that did not trust anyone. They wanted to make all decisions themselves. They did not want anybody who could make their own decisions because it might be wrong and then they would have to do it themselves. They consciously or unconsciously selected the very weakest people as their direct reports. They were so weak, they had to bring all decisions to this particular leader, which made him happy, but it also made him a weak leader as he was not able to develop leadership skills in those people below him. We look for leaders who surround themselves with competent people and if possible, are even smarter and better than they are. That makes them look better.

"The employee has the ability to go into a firestorm and solve issues" is the next statement. Firestorms are clients who are upset about something. Firestorms are potential issues that have to be addressed, like labor relation problems. When we have employees who can independently go into these situations and solve them, the more senior leaders do not have to stop what they are doing to get involved with the process. This is one of the most valuable skillsets of any MOLE employee.

The MOLE scores are ranked from 1 to 7, with 1 being the lowest and 7 the highest. We are looking for people that come in at a level 5 or above. That is a person that is functioning exactly the way you want them to function at a very high level, and everything is going well. If they are functioning to a level not quite that good, we would rank them a 4. It's not bad enough you would discipline them, but they aren't at the level you want them. An example of this is punching in at the time clock. Let's say the guidelines are employees must punch in seven minutes before or seven minutes after the hour. What you really want are people that punch in four or five minutes before their hour, so they can be prepared, at their desk, and ready to go to work on the hour. If they punch in four or five minutes after the hour it's not bad enough you would discipline them, but you're not happy about it either. If you rank them a 4, it allows you to talk about the issue and why you do not believe they deserve a 5. The time clock issue may improve over the next three-month period. If they are functioning so bad it's a 3, that is going to require a plan of correction. As you get down to 1 or 2 there may be discipline involved with the plan of correction. 6s are given to people who are truly outstanding. We have a number of outstanding employees in our company. 7s are rare, but they do exist. A 7 is about as perfect as an employee can be in that particular area you are evaluating. As we mentioned earlier, once you have all of your employees evaluated with MOLE scores you can put them on a scoreboard where you can see at a glance who needs your help and in what area.

Job Description Review

The next major area is a numerical evaluation of their job description checklist. As you read through the job description of any staff member, you will start to pick up very specific duties for which they are responsible. For example, if you had a Legal Manager over contracts, you may use a checklist similar to our example below, built off of their job description:

1. Manage outside counsel and litigation across entire territory
2. Provide monthly legal department metrics to the appropriate team members
3. Travel for trials, deposition, and mediation as necessary

4. Organize the company annual legal summit
5. Train industry professionals at least six times annually
6. Conduct annual company training for employees
7. Develop at least one marketable training lecture per year
8. Manage case reviews
9. Handle RFPs
10. Contracts
11. Strategic Planning
12. Communication
13. Execution
14. Overseeing salaries
15. Overall staff management
16. Client relations

You may notice your job descriptions are far too generalized and therefore neglect the specific job duties and times estimates needed to accurately assess and employee's status. If so, you should start by having a time study done by the employee. This is a week long process where they write down every single thing they do to include answering the phone (list topics discussed) and cleaning up the conference room following a meeting. We notice after a time study, employees become a bit surprised by exactly how many tasks they have absorbed under the "all other duties" category.

After the week long time study, the employee can expand on the job duties list to write down those specific tasks they have done and how long it takes them to do it (approximately) each week/month/etc. That is the list they should be reviewed on in coaching through a number score. When all of these are done, the numbers are averaged, and a final number is given which can then be put on a spreadsheet or scoreboard for you to see who is functioning at the highest level on their job description and who needs help.

Execution is a new area we have started to review. People have a lot of action items that come out of various meetings. The question is, do they get them done correctly and in the expected timeframe? Do they execute? Not everyone does. You can keep numerical records of this and see who is and is not completing their action items. For example, if a person has ten action items, and by the second meeting of the month they only have completed two, that would give them a 20 percent (2/10) score of completion for execution. Added to that is their commitments for the week. If they had two commitments and both were completed, that would raise their score to a 33 percent (4/12).

That score is then taken to the next week and we look at the number then. We keep track of all of the complete and incomplete items and at the end of the three month period we can look at "execution score" to see if a person completes what they say they are going to complete.

The next area we review is any significant problems with which our MOLE employee has had to deal. For example, if they had an employee who was not performing and they had to do extensive training, we expect them to follow up with a "2/4/6 program" (discussed in depth in Chapter 3) and keep written records of the problem for report at the coaching meetings. There may be four or five programs over the last three months with which they had to work. It is important to review this with the employee because it will give you an idea of how they think and work. It also tells you what problems they have been working on.

Next is budget review. How is the leader managing their particular budget? Are they saving or bleeding money? How is their staffing? Are they using supplies appropriately or overusing? Is their travel budget being managed properly? These are complicated questions and frequently must be answered by the particular leader in consultation with the accounting department and their immediate superior. Unfortunately, there are leaders who may think about "work" all the time, but not necessarily think about the budget for which they are responsible.

The next area reviewed are the individual goals of the employee. Individual goals are critical because if you take all of the goals from all of the senior staff, they form a massive network and actual road map of precisely how the company is going to achieve the vision and mission statements. The goals come out of the individual's personal mission statement, which was written from the company's mission statement. It should all flow together. Review each individual goal with the leader and again look at it for appropriateness. Is it measurable and is it time sensitive? Review the latest update for each particular goal and note if it is on track to be completed in the timeframe allowed. Are there goals that have been completed and can be removed? Are there new goals to be added? A detailed review of the goals is critical to understanding this employee's ability to execute.

The next area is reviewing new action items that were created during this meeting. Finally, a concluding paragraph or two about how you feel overall the employee is doing. Remember coaching at this level is never a report card or a "gotcha"— it is meant entirely to help the employee become stronger and better at their jobs. It should be an uplifting and interesting discussion. Always endeavor to keep it positive and keep the employee focused on constant improvement.

After the face-to-face interview is done, you need to fill out the lengthy coaching form and finish by recording a brief summary for both individuals to retain. Always be positive and uplifting while reinforcing the points you want to change from a behavioral standpoint.

Strategic Manual for Job Positions

We recommend every position in your organization have a strategic manual that outlines their job. When you open the binder it should be divided out by the job description, the job functions and time estimates, BUS plan, goals, and forms for additional tasks added since last review and BUS plans in process.

The job description allows the employee and the supervisor to agree to the role that is being filled. This has more human resources comments on it about the needs of the position and qualifications needed. You may have things on there about their Department of Labor (DOL) FLSA (Fair Labor Standards Act of 1938) categories and travel expectations.

The job functions and time estimates page allows the employee to share all of the details of the job they are doing and about how long it takes to do them. From this page metrics should be built. When an employee estimates taking calls requires about 3 hours/day and their metrics creep up to an average of 6 hours/day, they have a data backed basis to ask their supervisor to help them in prioritizing, offloading tasks (by flexing into their BUS plan – explained later) or finding another solution to correct the issue.

The next tab is the BUS plan and takes the most work to prepare. The BUS plan is the step by step guide of what someone would need to do in order to perform the task if you were injured (by a bus) or unable to perform your work for any reason (such as other tasks taking priority). Some tasks will be very clear with how to draft up the step by step; other tasks will need to be drafted in a way to point someone in the general direction of how to accomplish the task. That is okay. Identifying the person who will need to accomplish the task is another recommended action to add.

Next, add in the purpose, vision, company and department missions to the manual. From this, the employee should build their goals for the year along with metrics to track them. This allows coachings to review the status they are at in reaching their goals.

This manual is intended to be a living document to be updated at a minimum of each quarter (typically at coaching). Therefore, we recommend additional pages be added that will remind employees to add additional job duties they find themselves completing. Also a page regarding BUS plans to show which BUS plans they are flexing into for themselves or whose BUS plans they are on (or actively covering).

Creating these for the first time is a big undertaking. Start with the time estimates and job functions. Roll back to refining the job description topics off of that. Then write the BUS plan details. Keep this all in a binder and write in notes as the weeks go by. Update it formally with human resources quarterly. Used in the manner we recommend will not only allow an employee to track their work and monitor it to show how well they are doing, but it will also allow a supervisor to identify when they need to build in infrastructure for growth. Finally, doing this will help human resources and coworkers cover tasks if a position is unexpectedly open and requires coverage. Creating this system is a perfect indication of strategic planning in action.

Chapter Pearls

- Coach employees using positive and informative discussions
- Do not use annual reviews; coach regularly
- Use your tools (CAMPS-T, MOLE Test, job task rankings, execution score, budget review and action item list)
- Document coaching interactions
- Create strategic plan manuals for positions

| 13 |

Monitoring as a MOLE Leader

Leaders serve many important and interrelated functions. On any given day, a supervisor may be expected to meet with clients, hire new staff, train, and a whole host of other tasks. Even new leaders can be called on to accomplish a great deal of important business on behalf of the company. In order to extend a leader's sphere of influence, it is critical they become experts at monitoring their direct reports for compliance with company standards. This is made all the more important by the fact we must often manage projects remotely, without actually being there. There are a number of concepts leaders have to master to be successful at this task.

Monitoring employee behavior is part of a leadership process which includes assigning a task, training the employee to meet the standard, resourcing the employee with appropriate tools to be successful, evaluating, and applying lessons learned. Though it can seem like a big challenge, it becomes more manageable once a leader understands a few concepts and processes. This chapter will seek to make those concepts and processes understandable.

You Inspect What You Expect

More than any other phrase, perhaps this best sums up monitoring employees in a single concept. Think about this phrase for a minute and reflect on what it is saying. You inspect what you expect. Though it may seem simplistic, it is a concept that is frequently overlooked by new leaders. It is simply a clever way to say, if a leader does not check on a task, an employee will most likely forget about the task. This does not mean they are bad employees. Like all of us, our employees are busy. They will seek to make their life easier by not spending time on unimportant tasks. Since you are not inspecting this particular task, the staff will rightly assume it is not important to you and therefore may not need to be completed.

It is not difficult to see this concept in action in our company. For instance, if a manager does not invest time into reviewing proper documentation, an employee will assume the documentation is unimportant to their supervisor, and they will be unlikely to invest any significant effort into the task. This will result in sloppy documentation that could become extremely problematic if the documentation is reviewed for legal purposes. Conversely, if a manager puts a lot of effort into training an employee on the proper expectation and routinely follows up with the employee to assess their performance in this area, the employee will be aware of the importance of this task. As long as they have been trained properly and they understand the importance, they will excel in this area. If they do not, then you have the wrong person for the job.

Ensuring employees have been trained properly and understand the importance is a key concept here. A MOLE leader does not tell an employee they are doing it wrong and to do better. A MOLE leader works to find the reason why the employee is neglecting the behavior they want to see and works to determine how they can help the employee succeed moving forward. The MOLE leader should feel confident the employee has learned the material and the expectation at the end of their interaction and knows how they will be reviewed on it in the future. What type of inspection should they expect moving forward, and what would the MOLE leader like to see moving forward? Without guidance and inspection, old habits will return, and the employee will be left feeling confused and untrained. Leaders always have to remember the message they send with their supervision and monitoring of tasks. They inspect what they expect.

The Science of Degradation

Many years ago, it was identified by medical leadership that patients returning to incarceration were at a higher risk of suicide attempt. In an effort to save lives, leadership met and came up with a communication plan to alert clients and employees of triggers, risks, and how to implement precautions. The problem went away. Years later, the problem seemed to return. After investigating the issue, leadership realize the communication plan was no longer being followed. They were left with the question: What happened?

Process degradation is circular. A problem is identified and a team works to come up with a solution. The solution, or "perfect process", is communicated and implemented and the problem goes away. However, time goes by and the problem returns. Process degradation is linked to the quality and stability of a system. The decay can occur through several means, such as staff turnover or someone finding an "easier way" who was unaware of the reason behind the process. Regardless of the cause, entire organizations, staff and patients can be impacted by a single process' degradation.

Why do perfect systems degrade over time? Staff working a process that they were not involved in creating may believe they see a "better way". Their way may be seem easier, faster, and fit better into their schedule. The problem arises when they alter or remove pieces of a process that impact the end goal without understanding the reason behind the rule/process/plan. If a medical team, for example, independently decides it is easier to have all communication with custody to go through one nurse, what happens when that nurse is out of the facility? What happens when a patient returns from court and that nurse is on paid time off? The answer is degradation - the vital information is missed and the process begins to degrade. Lives may be lost due to finding "a better way".

Another way the "perfect process" may degrade is through poor training. Staff need to understand the reasons behind the rules they are expected to uphold. The "slack in the screw" concept (explained in this book) is a problem that arises when information is assumed to be intuitive. Every step of a process must be documented and trained on. If a medical team, for example, had simply been told to communicate with custody staff about court outcomes, they may not recognize that the conversation is a trigger to action based upon the information. Teams must communicate and train on even the things that seems obvious to them. To others, it may not be so obvious.

Turnover is a significant area in which preventable process degradation occurs. Each time you hire new staff, processes must be fully explained (the reason why) and effectively trained. The assumption that new staff understand your processes due to other education or experience is incorrect. Consider a situation where training is put off and a new employee is hired under an untrained manager. You cannot have the untrained leading the untrained. This will lead you down a path of degradation.

In 2023, a medical study entitled "It Takes an Average of 17 Years for Evidence to Change Practice - the Burgeoning Field of Implementation Science Seeks to Speed Things Up" found exactly that - it takes 17 years to change a practice. The cycle of degradation can be stopped by inspecting what you expect (a concept explained in this book). This process involves beginning with a training that explains expectations, the reasons behind the rules, and documents the understanding of staff. This process is then monitored by a leader who is clear about what they will be inspecting and expecting. The leader is not trying to catch staff making mistakes - they are there to provide insight, assistance, and resources as needed to make sure the process remains intact and effective.

Formal retraining should take place at seven and at thirty-day increments after the initial implementation to prevent staff from forgetting nearly 97% of what has been trained, a concept called the Curve of Forgetting. This is also an opportunity to catch any "earthworms" (a concept explained in this book)- which could be people subverting a process because it is causing them pain in some area. Consider if the medical and custody teams were not on good terms, so over time they began to limit their interactions and not speak to one another. This would cause the specific breakdown of communication and lives could be lost. This earthworm issue would need to be resolved by retraining on the reason behind the rule and/or changing out teams if necessary.

Finally, the process should be monitored over time on a minimum of a quarterly basis during coaching. This is when a BUS plan or strategic plan manual (a concept explained in this book) is reviewed to make sure every step is being followed in the manner in which it was intended.

Remote Monitoring

MOLE managers are experts at monitoring their facilities remotely. This is accomplished in a number of ways, but perhaps the most important tool to use is simple follow up calls.

During onsite visits, you should be able to develop an understanding of the particular weaknesses and strengths of each member of your team. For instance, you may have found during your inspection an employee does not understand how to properly collect data statistics. Of course, you should take the time to conduct training at the site while you are there—and appropriately document the training—however, simply training is not enough. You should also monitor by follow-ups.

In this example, you can schedule a follow up call for two days later to ensure the training and improvements are still functioning. If there are any new issues, those can be addressed at that time. A couple of days later, another call is made to check in and ensure the process is becoming a habit. After a few forced check-ins, a more customized version of the 2/4/6 plan (discussed in depth in the chapter on Training the MOLE) can be created to maintain the appropriate functioning of the task.

During the calls, simply ask how the data collection is going. The employee should be able to tell you a pretty straightforward answer. If they cannot answer simply, it may be because they have not put any effort into addressing the issue. If your intuition tells you this is the case, you could ask them to go ahead and send you their data so you can review and offer feedback. This reinforces the message it is important, and also makes them accountable for their actions. This is just one example. Routine training and follow up calls should be the norm at most of your sites, especially in those where the staff may be struggling to meet the standard.

Cadence of Monitoring

In their book *The 4 Disciplines of Execution*, Chris McChesney, Sean Covey, and Jim Huling describe the second discipline as lead indicators. The third discipline is scoreboarding, and the fourth is cadence. These are the main areas you need to focus on when monitoring your projects. Think about what lead indicators you need to monitor on a regular basis and benchmark all of your sites against this. This will show you which sites are strongest and weakest. For example, you could benchmark completed documentation or appropriate ordering of supplies. This will help you to understand where a particular site compares to others for which you have responsibility. These indicators will then go on a scoreboard you can share with your sites when you visit. This will help them to understand where they are relative to others.

The cadence is the frequency in which each meeting is conducted. In our company for client meetings we start with a phone call to the staff and to administration the first month to reassure ourselves things are going okay. The second month, we do an onsite visit, followed by a letter. The third month we do a telephone call to staff and administration. The fourth month we do a quality audit. Constantly maintaining this cadence with a touch at least once a month will ensure you are adequately monitoring your sites.

We have many routine meetings in our company. There is, for example, the Monday staff meeting, which is primarily for communication and to review on a regular basis where the company stands on all of its goals. Other examples include the training meeting and retention meeting. Each department has their own specific meetings. It is critical during this time you maintain consistent timing of these meetings so people can plan their time and ensure they are getting all of their action items and commitments down for these very important meetings.

A lot of the examples in this section have been guided toward medical and health care employees, but the principals are true for all leaders. As a MOLE leader you should always develop a system of lead indicators and scoreboarding to help you monitor your staff. You should have meetings on a regular basis to establish the cadence of monitoring that will give you the best results.

As you read the book *The 4 Disciplines of Execution*, it talks about measures or ways to monitor your progress. You can see what you focus on is what is going to get done. You have to set up ways to measure metrics. They talk about lag metrics and lead metrics. A lead metric is when you say, "I need to, as a sales person, sell more of the product." You know if you call ten prospective clients a day, you may get one appointment. That is thirty appointments a month, and if you get thirty appointments a month, you will get the opportunity to write maybe three contracts, and out of that you will close one contract. That is twelve contracts a year and will meet everything you need to do. You see you can measure this because it is a lead metric or goal. Every day you can see if you have done your job. If you are not completing it, you better pump it up a little bit. You are not working hard enough, you let the whirlwind get you, or something happened to slow you down.

The lag goal is to look back at the end of a quarter and see how many contracts you actually landed. You only landed two contracts. The second quarter you only landed one contract. Now you have to go back and look at your lead goal, are ten calls a day enough? Do you need to call fifteen a day, because it is directly related to how many potential clients you close? This is the difference between a lead and a lag metric.

Chapter Pearls

- Inspect what you expect
- Maintain a monitoring and communication cadence
- Use 2/4/6 programs

| 14 |

Strategic Planning for the MOLE Leader

Strategic planning is simply thinking about the future. It is done in a very structured fashion. It begins with you deciding how you want your world to look five years from now, and then writing down in a single sentence a brief description of what that would look like (vision). This is followed by a more complex mission statement describing how you are going to achieve your vision, followed by multiple goals designed to achieve all of the things needing to be accomplished to complete the mission and achieve the vision.

Understanding the importance of goal setting and how to do goal setting is vital to your growth as a MOLE leader. In this chapter, we will be referring to the book *The 4 Disciplines of Execution* by Chris McChesney, Jim Huling, and Sean Covey. We will explain why we use this book to guide us in goal setting.

A Road Map to Success for the MOLE Leader

A MOLE leader works to develop and follow a clear road map to success. This is the corporate strategic plan. At our company the department directors, vice presidents, and above meet for an entire week in October. In the month leading up to the meeting, projections concerning next year's sales goals with estimates of increased numbers of contracts and employees are handed out to the appropriate departments. This allows everyone to be prepared with their own set of goals to meet the increased workload that will be developed over the next 12-month period. The meetings start early on Monday morning with a clear review of where we are in our present five-year plan and detailed analysis of the exact financial situation. All information, good and bad, is shared with all leaders. There are no secrets. During this early discussion, successes and challenges are shared. Honesty is the rule. In addition to our clear strategic plan, the company usually has three or four initiatives we are specifically working on. There is a detailed analysis and report on these initiatives in the early program. From there we move on to an open and honest discussion of our **S**trengths, **W**eaknesses, **O**pportunities, and serious **T**hreats to the company (SWOT analysis). During these discussions there is frequently a rearrangement of the items on SWOT. At times we add more strengths or possibly remove items we thought were opportunities that did not turn out for us. At the end of the meetings, each leader is responsible for communicating their individual goals for the upcoming year.

What is a Vision?

Consider for a moment a football team as a corporation. At the beginning of the season, the entire team can see themselves standing in the middle of the field at the Super Bowl, holding the trophy above their heads and cheering. They can visualize it. It is the beginning of the year and it has not happened yet. The coaches do not know exactly how they are going to accomplish this, so they need to create a plan. The team had the vision. The image they have forms the basis of a vision statement because they can see this happening. They know when the Super Bowl is, but they do not yet know how they are going to win. The coaches have to figure out what to do to make it happen. Senior management gathers the coaches and everyone involved and writes a road map in order to accomplish this vision. The vision is, "standing in the middle of the field, holding up the trophy."

What is a Mission?

Now that the team has their vision decided, they need to decide what they can do to accomplish that vision. What mission do they have to take on? This can be different department to department, but the overall mission is the pull in the same direction.

The offensive coach says, "What we're going to do is to score more points than the opposing teams." This is their mission, "score more points."

The defensive coach says, "We're going to prevent the other teams from scoring as many points as we score." This is their mission, to "prevent points."

The people who are in charge of the assistance and rehab say, "We're going to prevent injuries, and keep our players equipped and on the field."

Everybody comes up with their mission and it is all put it into one common statement they are all going to accomplish. One little paragraph of what they are going to do. That is the corporate mission. Now we all know what we are going to do. The mission is: *To score more points than our opponents, to stop the other team from scoring as many points as we do, to reduce injuries and supply all of the equipment needed.*

The truth of the matter is not everybody can do everything. The offensive coach does not really understand defense, so he cannot write any goals for defense. The defensive coach does not understand offense, so he cannot write any goals for offense. What they have to do is look at the mission statement and pull out the things they can do.

The offensive coach says, "I have to score more points than the other team, so how am I going to get that done? What do I have to achieve in order to get that done?" He begins to think about this and writes his own personal mission statement on how he is going to accomplish the one thing that is in the corporate mission. Then he takes the mission statement and breaks it down into the subunits and says, "In order to score more points we have to have a higher rate of passing. So how are we going to get that done? I will write a goal for more passing and we will set up training and plans to accomplish this." He then goes through all the various goals he has to achieve. That is what vision, mission, and goal setting is all about. Everyone can do it.

Strategic Plan Meetings

How do we do it? Every year in October the directors get together for a week and look at the corporate vision, which is a very small, simple thing, but is a very legalistic instrument because it tells us exactly what we have to do. Each word is very important. As a group, we look at it and update it every year. These were the ACH purpose, vision, and mission statements in 2019:

SAMPLE PURPOSE STATEMENT

The purpose of ACH is to solve problems and make lives easier.

SAMPLE VISION

Advanced Correctional Healthcare, Inc. cares for the underserved by delivering a higher standard of correctional health care through professionalism, integrity, commitment, and problem solving.

SAMPLE MISSION

ACH leads the industry with professionalism, integrity, and adherence to higher standards in medical care, mental health care, and business services. We are committed to recruiting, training, developing, and retaining an expert team of professionals empowered to solve problems and do the right thing. Strategic planning, clear communication, and strong partnerships facilitate the efficient delivery of services that enhance patient, client, and employee satisfaction. Our success is achieved by research, analysis, customized solutions, and proactive monitoring.

In 2019, we changed our vision and mission statements because we did not think they said enough about problem-solving. As you look at the corporate vision, you can see a major problem. It is not exciting and does not really explain what we do or the real purpose of the company. The corporate vision is simply a legal instrument that defines how we need to proceed over the next five years. We developed a purpose statement that clearly stated what each of us and the company really does.

When we started to think about what it is we really do, we solve problems. That's the whole thing we do. Not only do we do that corporately, but we do it individually, so every one of our staff was hired to solve a problem. All day long they solve problems. Who do we do that for? Well, we are doing it for our patients, for our clients, and for ourselves, our employees. Because we all need to solve problems for each other, we all need to make our lives easier as we go through our daily work.

These legalistic instruments are very structured. Every word is important. Everybody in the company should look at this statement and determine what they can do to help the company accomplish the mission. If you can do that, you will hit the vision, purpose will be accomplished, and your company will all be happy.

Word of the Year

Upon finalizing the vision, mission, and purpose, the word of the year should be discussed. This is the one word the entire company will focus on for the year. In the early years of the company, the word of the year was very motivating and emotional. Words like "survive" gave leaders the focus and drive to sell contracts and follow through on their word. Now that we are two decades into the organization, words have evolved into our necessary maintenance and improvements. Words like "training" and "execution" have been used in order to develop training systems and to make sure staff are executing the things they set out to do.

Each word of the year is expected to be used in a minimum of one goal per leader. Therefore, if the word is training, it would not be uncommon for a manager to make a goal to train their staff annually on a certain task. That would accomplish the focus for the year for that person. Another version may be a leader who makes a goal to get trained on an item they feel deficient in. Both goals are aimed at training. Upon deciding the word of the year, it is time for leaders to conduct an honest SWOT analysis.

Honest SWOT Analysis

SWOT analysis is a tool to evaluate your strengths, weaknesses, opportunities, and threats to the company. We conduct an in-depth SWOT analysis four times a year, analyzing the market and the new shifting winds of opportunity and threats that come at all companies.

The entire senior management of the company is involved and asks themselves the question, "What are the strengths of this company?" Strengths are defined as those company qualities that are superior to any of your competitors. This honest appraisal will help define who you are and what you do well. It is particularly important for your business development department because they can frequently use this in their marketing material. The strengths must be honest, truthful, and recognized by all. One good way to document your strengths is to survey your clients. Their feedback will direct you on true strengths.

Our client survey included statements scored on a 1-7 scale such as:

1. Advanced Correctional Healthcare (ACH) demonstrates integrity.
2. ACH demonstrates professionalism.
3. ACH demonstrates reliability.
4. ACH is responsive when I have a problem.

There were many other statements in our marketing firm's survey, but we believe you get the idea by looking at these few.

Some years ago, we hired a marketing firm to help us develop some marketing material. They asked us what the strengths were that our clients had identified in us. We gave them our list of answers, and they immediately went out and surveyed all of our clients for those specific answers. They concluded we were absolutely accurate. Our assessment of our strengths was the same as our clients' assessment of our strengths. This indicated we were being honest to ourselves and were not fooling ourselves about our talents and abilities. Armed with that material, the marketing team was able to develop a new marketing strategy that helped us even more. Each quarter as we repeat our SWOT analysis and look at our strengths, we bring the strengths from the last quarter forward and ask ourselves if there are new strengths we can identify or if some of our strengths have been gained by our competitors such that they are no longer unique to us. Spirited discussion occurs on each of the strengths identified. As we go through our discussions, these words are added or subtracted from a master list on the big screen in front of us, so everyone can see where we are at any time in the discussion.

When we are satisfied we have identified all of our major strengths we move to weaknesses. For me this is far more important than strengths, because it tells us those areas we must focus on with action items. Weaknesses are defined as those operations in the company we do not perform as well as our competitors or as well as we believe we are capable of operating. Examples of weaknesses could be the percent of turnover of staff and we need a plan to reduce it, or maybe our HR department is having trouble getting new hire paperwork completed when people are hired in a distant state. Each quarter all of the weaknesses from the prior quarter are brought forth and each one is individually analyzed along with action items to correct or improve the situation. It is these action items that are critically important to execute change.

Opportunities are the next area of discussion. Here we're looking for those opportunities in which we have not capitalized. For example, the rise in the opioid crisis in the United States has created opportunities for treatment programs that could be used by each of our clients to help their underserved patient population. Since we had not developed specific programs, this was an opportunity and action items had to be written to push us in the direction of program development and then marketing an entire new line of products. Opportunities is a particularly exciting part of SWOT analysis because it opens the door for your company to move in new directions previously unconsidered.

Threats are the last part of the SWOT analysis we look at. A threat is defined as a potential problem that could literally take the company down. This could be a catastrophic lawsuit, a new report that has come out on a particular product you provide that is negative, or a news article exposé about your company or the company's leadership. Each threat must be dealt with as a potential catastrophic event, and all resources must be mobilized to reduce or get rid of these threats and move them to weaknesses or areas that would not "take the company down."

Once you have completed your SWOT analysis you should have a fairly lengthy list of action items assigned to specific people who are responsible complete them within a specific time frame. These action items need to be moved to your weekly meetings so they are reviewed very frequently and everyone knows where you stand on all action items. In the end, we should have an action item for each weakness, opportunity, and threat to the company. These action items will each be assigned to one individual person and will be reported on weekly in our Monday meetings for the next year or until they are resolved.

When our SWOT analysis is complete, we are prepared to go back to the beginning and look at the purpose of the company. Is our purpose properly worded to guide us throughout the balance of the five-year plan? We have set up a system of yearly strategic plans with five-year overall goals. Once the five-year goals are established, they generally do not change for the next five years. By watching the metrics and measuring every three months, we can ensure we are on track to achieve the five-year goal. The exact wording of the purpose statement and the vision statement is critical to the direction and longevity of the company. An improperly worded statement will restrict your ability to head in a different direction when the market is changing.

Advanced Buggy Whips, Inc.

Consider for a moment you are the CEO of Advanced Buggy Whips, Inc., a company that makes the finest buggy whips in America.

Your purpose statement is: *The purpose of Advanced Buggy Whips, Inc., is to provide American carriage drivers with the finest instrument to help control and guide their horses.* The vision statement is: *Advanced Buggy Whips, Inc., is a successful company providing stylish products for the discerning carriage driver.*

The year is 1905 and automobiles are just coming onto the market. In ten years, the buggy whip market will plummet, but because you have locked yourself in to a purpose and vision statement that does not allow you to look outside of your normal range of business, you may not be able to move quickly to take advantage of new opportunities. If your purpose statement was more in line with: *The purpose of Advanced Buggy Whips, Inc., is to provide the instruments to assist drivers as they guide their vehicles down American roads.*

We believe you can see that as automobiles came on board you could diversify into gas pedals and carburetor linkages. The point is you would not be driven into a corner that was slowly dying out. As you review the vision statement for Advanced Buggy Whips, Inc., removal of one word allows you to broaden your marketable products. For example: *Advanced Buggy Whips, Inc. is a successful company providing stylish products for the discerning driver.*

Simply removing the word carriage allows you to move into automobiles. We understand this example may seem a little simpleminded, but the problem is very real. The importance of properly wording purpose and vision statements is critical. Every year we look at our purpose and vision statements and we develop a mission statement for the company that will drive us forward for at least the next 12 months. We are always looking at the estimated growth of the company, which has been provided to us a month prior to the meeting by business development.

The mission statements change little from one year to the next, but they do occasionally have to be modified based upon our understanding of our goals, values, and various market forces we were unaware of in the previous year. When the corporate mission statement is completed each vice president, director, and other senior officers write their own mission statements by pulling specific items out of the corporate mission statement.

Once we have completed a purpose statement, vision statement, and mission statement, we now have to ask ourselves, are our core values adequate to help us accomplish those things we must complete?

Company Core Values

It is important to understand most companies have a set of core values. Usually these are three to five various values which typically include integrity and honesty. We recommend a far more aggressive program of core values. We are currently using 20+ separate core values. Some are listed below.

1. Professionalism: Acts and behaves appropriately in appearance and manner
2. Integrity: Having an honest and trustworthy character
3. Commitment: Dedicated to goals or activities consistent with the values of ACH
4. Problem Solving: Identifies and acts on problems to achieve appropriate solutions
5. Accountability: Answerable for behaviors and outcomes
6. Collaboration: Works productively with others to achieve a shared goal
7. Communication: Clearly, intentionally, and effectively exchanges information or news and provides feedback
8. Composure: The ability to control oneself, particularly one's emotions or the expression of them in one's behavior, especially in difficult situations

9. Courtesy: Displays politeness in attitude and behavior toward others
10. Dependability: Consistent and reliable in all aspects of behavior and action
11. Diligence: Displays a constant and earnest effort to accomplish what is undertaken
12. Discretion: Behaves and speaks in a way to avoid revealing private information and to respect confidentiality
13. Empathy: Recognize and acknowledge others' feelings
14. Flexibility: Willing and able to adapt to a rapidly changing environment
15. Initiative: Handles needs without being directed
16. Interpersonal Relations: Able to develop strong, personal relationships with employees and clients
17. Job Skills: Has the ability to complete assigned tasks in an organized manner with attention to detail
18. Leadership: Ability to lead, guide, and direct employees with our value-based system
19. Loyalty: Displays faithfulness to ACH, staff, and clients
20. Optimism: Takes a favorable or confident view
21. Ownership: Taking personal responsibility for duties or tasks
22. Receptiveness: Accepts and applies constructive feedback positively
23. Respectfulness: Treats others with positive consideration and regard
24. Responsiveness: Takes action in a timely manner
25. Strategic Planning: Anticipates needs and creates a plan to accomplish a goal
26. Work Ethic: Displays a set of values based on hard work

Most companies will suggest you cannot have more than three to five core values because people cannot focus on more than that. We suggest that 26 is a reasonable number if you use them on a daily basis.

In MOLE leadership core values are used to evaluate people in 360s and to recognize people for the qualities of their personality and character that help drive the company forward. For example, one of our core values is flexibility. Flexibility is important to the company because in the medical field we must be staffed according to the guidelines of our clients. If someone becomes ill and cannot come to work, we need someone to cover. If a vacation is coming up and someone will be out for a week, we need staff who will step in and cover. It is not uncommon that we will have an employee who will go out of their way to cover for people when they must be gone from their jobs. Because of this they are given recognition certificates for flexibility. In the certificate the story is told about what they did so a clear description of the behavior demonstrating flexibility is described. The award is for demonstrating the core value of flexibility. We track the thank-you's and certificates given for each core value and can tell which core values are the most important from the standpoint of helping our team provide the necessary services.

As mentioned earlier, 360s are also performed throughout the company using core values. Each core value has at least one or two questions specific to it. Each question has a 1-7 rating with 7 being the best and 1 being the worst on how this individual demonstrates those particular values. This is the same scale mentioned in the CAMPS-T section where we referenced the timeclock.

Now that the group has determined the vision, mission, purpose, word of the year, strengths, weaknesses, opportunities, threats, and values for the company, each leader gets their chance to speak. They share their goals for the upcoming year and how they may be further modified to meet any adjustments made in the days leading up to their presentation. They suggest ways they can add a goal to meet the needs of the word of the year, and how their specific department will support the company.

How to Create Goals

The problem is this: one person cannot do everything in the mission. So, we trade up our thoughts. Here is how to do it for the role of CEO. Review the corporate mission and identify how many areas for which the CEO is responsible. Higher standards of medical care, you can work on that, can't you? Teaching and training, you can write goals on those. Business services, you do some of that. Developing, retaining an expert team of professionals, now you have a little bit to do with that, because you get to determine salaries and benefits. Customized programs, you do that because you develop a lot of programs. Research, you get involved with research. Monitoring, you need to do that. Next, literally take a yellow marker and mark the things for which you are responsible. Now bring these together and write a personal mission statement. Out of that mission statement, look to see how many items you have to do. From these write all of your goals. This is the mission statement:

CEO MISSION

The CEO leads the company with (1) strategic planning and (2) clear communication. They work to develop and retain an expert team of professionals with (3) good salaries and benefits and (4) the best training in the industry. (5) Personal relationships are maintained with key clients. All of this is completed with (6) higher business standards to ensure company success.

Go through the mission statement and decide how many items you have to accomplish. In this case, it turned out to be six different items. Next, number them. Then go to number one, strategic planning, and consider all the aspects of strategic planning. When you do this you cannot cover every single thing that should be done, but you can pick out one or two items that are measurable and time specific to build an entire goal based upon it. Since you meet with all of the senior staff quarterly for coaching sessions, that would be a good goal to achieve. Therefore write, "I will meet with every member of the senior team quarterly for a coaching session." This means you have to have specific plans and calendars laid out for the entire year to ensure this can be done. Under this goal a detailed list of plans can be developed, and a calendar attached so it is easy to see at any time if you are executing the goal. You said you needed to provide clear communication. That becomes goal number two. Good salaries and benefits becomes number three. The best training in the industry is number four. Personal relationships is number five. Higher business standards to ensure company success is number six. Under each goal there is a lengthy detailed list of the exact plans to accomplish the goals.

How do you write a goal? In this case we said, "All salaries and benefits will be reviewed and improved by the first week of December." It is time specific. Anybody could tell if you completed this goal, because you have to record what is accomplished during the year. Anyone could look at the goals and figure out if you are accomplishing your goals. That is how this whole process works.

You will be using a system of goals to guide you. Your goals should be in a manual you carry with you and work out of on a regular basis. You should keep your monitoring spreadsheets, scoreboards, and scorecards and all of the things you need in order to complete your goals. Ours is used as a workbook all the time, and is about a half inch thick. It includes all our documents and papers we use to monitor our daily activities. Every day we can tell you what we are doing, why we are doing it, and what goal is involved. You need to develop the same type of manual.

There are many different ways to write goals and it does not matter which way you choose to write them or track them as long as you are consistent and it works for you. The more people you talk to, the more people who will have opinions of their best practices, tips, and tricks. In the end, you need to commit to something that works for you and modify if it no longer serves the purpose you created it for. We recommend you write a personal mission statement based upon the mission statement from your division. You need to look at the division's mission statement and decide what you personally can do to contribute to that mission. You likely cannot do everything that is in there; but there are going to be pieces of things you do in your work within it. Your director will work with you to decide what goals you are going to have, do your goals make sense, are they measurable, and are they are all written correctly. This is the process you should use.

We have always had a system of goals to guide us since the company was founded. We always had a problem trying to get everyone pulling in the same general direction, the concept of pulling the particularly important goal (PIG). Then we stumbled across this book, *The 4 Disciplines of Execution*. It was wonderful because it recommended a system similar to ours, but it added things we had not thought about, so we could do it even better. That is why we use this book to this day to help our leaders grasp what it is we are doing and why we do it the way we do it.

HARD Goals

In *The 4 Disciplines of Execution*, McChesney, Huling, and Covey write that rule number 1 of focusing your organization is "no team can focus on more than two WIGs [wildly important goals] at the same time." Let us clear this up, because that is a little confusing. It might seem like you cannot have more than two goals, and we have eleven goals. Their WIG, their wildly important goal, is our PIG. We have one PIG. One particularly important goal, and that goal is to increase the bottom line in net profit by a set amount each year. That is the PIG. The PIG is the one goal every one of us needs to work on. It is absolutely critical. So, don't get confused when you see you can only work on one or two goals at a time, because that's true if you're talking about the big master issue you are trying to address. In the meantime, our goals are the legal instruments we use to structure ourselves and all of the goals we must achieve for the business.

When *The 4 Disciplines of Execution* discusses only working on one or two goals, they are speaking about the concept of HARD goals. HARD goals are a concept of goals that are Heartfelt, Animated, Required, and Difficult.

They are heartfelt because they are so important to you. They are animated, which means you can see them in your mind's eye and you can see this goal completed. They are required because if you do not get them done, something bad is going to happen. In addition, they are difficult. These are not easy things. That is a HARD goal. Now, the book will tell you that you can only have one or two HARD goals; remember we just said we have got eleven goals, but those are not HARD goals. Those are our daily work goals. Our goals help us understand what we have to do.

The best way to understand a HARD goal is to think about the goal Dr. Johnson had when he started this company. It was a HARD goal. He was the only doctor, we had eight clients, and we were in a negative cash flow. The goal that year was condensed down to one word: survival. He thought about surviving from the minute he got up in the morning until he went to bed at night. First thing the next morning he was thinking survival, how could he get this done, what could he do to get through the year. Then a project popped up that would help us. We landed that project and still remember the exact moment. It was animated because he thought about this all the time. He was the only doctor, he was required to be on the road five days a week, and if he didn't get this done he was going to go bankrupt. That pretty well had Dr. Johnson focused. It was hard. It was not easy. He had to take all calls, make all the decisions, and do everything.

That is a HARD goal. You may have something like that in your life —something you're just so focused on it absorbs what you're thinking and doing. If you wanted to look at a HARD goal at our company, our HARD goal would be our PIG, but truthfully, it is not nearly as important as that first year, which was survival. That is what a HARD goal is, be aware of that and as you come across it, do not get confused that you can only have one or two goals and then listen to goal guidance tell you that you have eleven or fifteen, or whatever you have got. They are different things.

Chapter Pearls

- Understand your purpose
- Meet annually with leaders
- Design a mission to achieve your vision
- Designs goals to achieve your mission
- Develop a word of the year to guide the organization
- Conduct an honest SWOT analysis
- Refine your company's values annually
- Develop goals to lead you

| 15 |

Recognizing the MOLE

"It's a simple truth: we work harder at places where we feel recognized and valued for our unique contributions. Recognizing and developing the potential of individuals is the real path to leadership."
– Adrian Gostick and Chester Elton, *The Carrot Principle*

Managers play a key role in developing the culture of your company. It is up to you as a manager to help create and develop the culture as you grow. The benefits should outweigh the cost of taking the time out of your day to recognize an employee or coworker. An important aspect of leadership is gauging your employees' satisfaction and engagement.

It is important to encourage and recognize employees for their efforts and achievements. Value-based recognition should give employees and coworkers a sense of value, while also potentially increasing employee retention, performance, and morale. Building a recognition program that recognizes employees for doing the work expected of them is a difficult concept for many managers to absorb. It is not the challenge of agreeing people should be thanked for the work they do, it is getting managers to take the time to stop what they are doing and write a thank you or pick up the phone to call someone. In many organizations, employees work side by side with their managers. A twenty second conversation to notify an employee that the manager heard a good thing about them and they appreciated the work they did that day goes a long way to creating loyalty and engagement. This type of behavior is completed with the goal of inspiring an employee to continue at a high level of performance, and to challenge those around them to model their behavior after the person being recognized.

If you have not read *The Carrot Principle* by Adrian Gostick and Chester Elton yet, please consider reading the book. As you read, you should notice the term "carrot" is used as a tool, or accelerant, and is used to inspire and motivate employees. Therefore, we support managers who encourage and inspire their employees to do better with recognition (carrots), rather than forceful demands for improvement. There is a difference between supporting and leading employees through recognition versus expecting and demanding through micromanaging. Employees should know the work they do has value in the company, and without them the company would be weaker in that area. When you recognize your employees, we advise against making jokes or making light of the situation. Recognition is serious and intentional.

Companies do not need a large budget to formalize a recognition program. It can be started without much monetary investment and grow as the company grows or as the program naturally evolves. Identifying one or two ways staff specific to your company want to be recognized and then doing it is a great way to begin. Thank-you notes are very common as well. Whether notes are sent via email, sticky notes, or texted, there are ways to initiate the program. Post signs to encourage the specific one or two recognition behaviors you want to trial to start and see how they catch on. Develop a team of three or four people to push the program and encourage people to use it, and also track or push out a survey to see how people are enjoying it. Modify from there. Our program did not become what it is today by jumping in the deep end. We started with thank-you notes and accepted feedback. We had a committee who pushed our intentions out, and then added a review of recognition (thank-you's) to employee coaching sessions. This is how we chose to inspect what we expected. From there, our program has grown into a large and robust program with a budget that allows for even client recognition.

Using what we've read from various recognition texts, we have developed a dynamic recognition program to encourage employees to be recognized for various reasons. Employees are recognized for exceptional work and their years of service (not seniority) from the start. Using terms such as "seniority" promotes a perception that performance is not paramount; instead, staying with a company is the only way to get special benefits. Recognizing for years of service specifically recognizes the action taken by the employee—remaining at the organization for a certain amount of time—rather than a superiority ranking by seniority. They are also recognized for various life and educational milestones. Marriages, children, hospital stays, deaths, and educational milestones all may have some sort of a recognition acknowledgment or gift. To participate in these forms or recognition, the employee or supervisor should notify human resources to initiate the recognition. There are also recognition practices for sites that have hardships or unexpected events occur. Again, supervisors initiate the recognition by contacting human resources.

Employees who want to thank their coworkers for something they did—for example, helping them catch up on sick calls or covering a shift—can immediately log online to send a thank-you note centered around the value the person exhibited to make their life easier. Leaders should use and encourage the use of thank-you notes to and from their employees. Every single day employees should be thanking each other for the day-to-day tasks they do. To encourage the program, we have decided five thank-you notes are worth $5 gift cards to many retailers across the U.S. and chosen by the individual who received them. Thank you notes should be flying from all levels of the organization to each other and back. The success of the thank-you note process is experienced when line level employees are thanking individuals across state lines after a consult or phone call. In the health care culture it appears collaboration is viewed as a job task, however it is not mandatory that individuals are nice to one another. Therefore, it is important to overcome the comments of "the person is just doing their job," and recognize the intention of recognition is to reinforce positive behaviors. Therefore, if someone completed medication pass correctly, they could be recognized that day for job skills or dependability for completing the task well.

Recognition Type:	Thank You Card
Core Value:	Collaboration
Date:	9/13/2019
From:	Angela Jones
To:	Jenifer Anderson
Thank you for being awesome!	

Recognition Type:	Thank You Card
Core Value:	Collaboration
Date:	9/13/2019
From:	Angela Jones
To:	Jenifer Anderson
Thank you for going out of your way to ask me if I needed help during the meeting. Because you offered to take minutes, I was able to troubleshoot the wi-fi issues on the spot. You made my life easier!	

The thank-you note should include why they are recognizing the individual, the specific value they are exhibiting, and a genuine thank-you. These should be timely and tied to a specific situation, not to a pattern of events that occurred over a long period of time. In this section you will see two example thank-you cards. One is written in an inadequate, nonspecific manner. Being "awesome" is not something a person can choose to continue, because there is no information to indicate what they did that was awesome. The other thank-you note outlines a properly written note that should engage the employee and serve as a carrot. Because of the specifics used, the individual knows exactly what behavior to continue in order to be recognized and create positive interpersonal relations.

Certificates

Sometimes a thank-you note is not formal enough to recognize the above and beyond action taken by an individual. It is more appropriate to thank an employee in front of a group of individuals and read a story about what occurred. In these instances, a certificate may be given. To begin writing a certificate, you should go to human resources and have them work with you to ensure you share the situation, what action the employee took, the impact on you or the organization as a result, and assign an appropriate value. You will then be scheduled to present the certificate at an upcoming event or function.

ADVANCED CORRECTIONAL HEALTHCARE, INC.

JOHN GREEN, REGIONAL NURSE MANAGER
recognizes
KOURTNEY WILLIAMS
FOR DEMONSTRATING THE VALUE OF
COMMITMENT

DEDICATED TO GOALS OR ACTIVITIES CONSISTENT WITH THE VALUES OF ACH

Recently, our client shared how happy they are with Nurse Williams as their Site Manager. Under her leadership, they have seen great improvement in the quality of their medical department. Nurse Williams has diligently worked to ensure the medical department works the way the jail intended, and identified opportunities for improvement – such as helping to change the facility's intake questionnaire. Specifically, the Captain appreciates Nurse Williams attitude and knowledge of the correctional healthcare industry, and ability to lead by example. Our client recognizes Nurse Williams as an asset to their department. Thank you, Nurse Williams, for your commitment to your site and our company. We appreciate you!

Date

Recognized by

Certificates are most impactful when being presented by the person who is giving the recognition or by someone who had direct contact in the situation being recognized. We understand various circumstances may arise in which a recognizer may be unable to present their certificate. For example, an out of state, part-time employee may wish to recognize the president as a result of something they received assistance with. Human resources will work with you on the unique situation you may be experiencing and set up a presentation in the most appropriate way.

Recognition may reinforce goal setting by rewarding commitments, action items, and employee goals that help achieve department goals. Recognition communicates to the entire company when someone makes a positive impact and highlights core values.

Awards and recognition items vary by event. Service awards, at this time, may come with either a certificate or an eagle statue with their name on it. Educational awards, depending on the milestone accomplished, may come with an educational initiative certificate and cash.

Of the Year Awards

In addition to service awards, life and educational milestones, thank-you notes and certificates, we have also established annual awards employees may be eligible to receive. As a general rule, we recommend you review your awards on a regular basis to determine if you will add, modify, or remove any. These are called "Of the Year" awards.

There is a Salesman of the Year, Qualified Mental Health Professional (QMHP) of the Year, Regional Nurse Manager of the Year, Nurse of the Year, Human Resources Professional of the Year, and Accounting Professional of the Year. Since the program began, this group of "Of the Year" awards come with a trophy, cash award, and two paid time off days. For these awards, we would like the winner to be able to have a long weekend away to thank them for their work and provide them with a bit of spending money. Again, they receive an award to remind them of their recognition upon returning to work. The awards in this category have defined expectations for the individuals who are eligible, such as goal completion, peer feedback, and other similar items.

Industry Specific Awards

In our organization, we have some industry specific awards that have developed over time. Individuals who have performed a lifesaving act in our company may be eligible for an engraved golden stethoscope or a lifesaver award. Awards should be mindfully chosen with the intent of it being a meaningful reward to the group of individuals recognized. What works for us will not work for every other company, even if it is a health care organization. Obtaining the award should set the individuals apart from others in a prestigious way, and the reason they received it should be a roadmap for others to know how to follow in their footsteps.

Our golden stethoscope award was created as a way to thank nurses who rise to their training and act in a time of crisis by performing CPR with a successful outcome of restoring a pulse. A stethoscope is a tool nurses use in their daily lives, and it relates to heart rate and breathing. Therefore, the golden stethoscope award was developed to allow nurses of this caliber to have a daily memory prompt of the successful outcome they created. After rolling out this award, we became aware nurses were not the only individuals performing CPR at the facilities, and we wanted to find a way to thank the correctional officers who also assist in life saving events. This evolved into a lifesaver award plaque in which officer names are added to show their successful efforts in life saving events. We are very grateful to be in partnership with such an essential and hardworking community of individuals.

Mini PIG

In our company, we recognize employees for assisting the company's stability through financial initiatives. Without employees, organizations will fail to deliver on the services they are created to address. Therefore, when an employee helps pull the company in the right direction by saving money without reducing services, that is called pulling the PIG (particularly important goal) in the right direction. This is not to be misconstrued with cutting services and costs haphazardly. This is about recognizing a waste in finances that may be better served spending in another area of the company. Therefore, if an employee finds a way to order orientation binders, for example, at a lesser rate by utilizing a different product or service, the employee is recognized for not only taking the time to think of this solution but also carrying it through to experience the savings. This is not something they have to do in their role, but instead, a selfless decision they made which will benefit other areas of the organization with the reduction in waste. When this savings is a minimum of a $250 over a year's time, the employee is given an award called the Mini PIG. All employees who receive a Mini PIG award during the year are eligible at the end of the year for the PIG award.

The PIG Award

At the end of the year, the total savings for each Mini PIG effort is calculated. The individual who reduced the most waste during the year is recognized with the PIG award. PIG winners have found ways to sign clients up for more efficient programs, show clients how to obtain discounts on daily use items, or educate practitioners on ways to consult more effectively with patients regarding medications. Without compromising care and with a focus on serving the underserved population in each community, the employees who win this award have spent time focusing on ways to help others.

The PIG Award is industry specific in health care because the prices of medications and supplies change quickly and often. Financial focus is on assisting clients with keeping the county money in the county and not being wasteful with taxpayer dollars for items that could be purchased in the same (or better) quality by adjusting brand name or process. It is important when developing a process like this that it is not deemed as a program of cutting quality or cost. The goal is not to pay less in any way possible. You do not want to impact quality because that behavior will trickle through your company by rewarding people for doing lesser quality work. Again, that is not the intention of a PIG Award. The intention is to reward people for being more innovative and seeking opportunities to do things more efficiently.

Professionalism Integrity Commitment (PIC) Award

Our organization also found value in creating an award that celebrates living the company core values in day-to-day life. We decided it had to be attainable by everyone in the organization, so we had to limit the focus on a few top values and open it to an annual vote. Choosing top values was not an easy task, but with time we determined if everyone in the organization had the top three or four values then we would forever be a great place to work.

The award became known as the PIC award, named after the top values chosen. The intent of this award is to recognize employees who live the company values throughout their tenure. It is given to one person who has exhibited Professionalism, Integrity, and Commitment to our company throughout the year in the eyes of their coworkers. The recipient is chosen based upon nominations from employees companywide. It does not matter what job title or location a person is from or how many hours they work, all employees company-wide are eligible to win. After an initial round of accepting nominations, the finalists are sent back out for a final round of voting. The intent of this award is to challenge employees of all levels to keep company values in the forefront of their mind and act with good intentions on a regular basis. Since the beginning of this program, both the PIG and the PIC awards have come with an engraved award, net cash and at least five paid time off days. The thought behind this prize package is to give the employee a week's paid vacation with some spending money. Then they have the award to remind them of their recognition upon return to work.

Our award format and structure will not work for every company or industry. You must create a culture that values recognition and find ways to recognize your employees based on the things that matter most to them. We hope to be able to inspire our employees to become engaged and strive to achieve company goals. Effective recognition should also help reduce turnover and enhance business results.

Recognition programs should be built in a dynamic way, which are able to make each individual person feel valued. Programs that recognize tenure (length of service) and life milestones or events (i.e., marriages, children, deaths, educational certificates/degrees) promote employee loyalty. Managers should be people who support employees during hardships or other events, and try to accommodate what is reasonably able during that time. MOLE employees need their manager's support, and managers should be able to communicate why the person is important to the company.

Companies lacking the funds to pay for a recognition program or for awards may find success in instituting a program of sending thank you notes. Recognition does not have to cost money. Employees could be encouraged to send thank-you notes to each other for "just doing their job," which should be tied to a personal value or personality aspect. The goal is to thank people for the things they do well, so they will continue to do that task. Thanking people does not cost money, but it is something that needs to be trained or it may not happen. Companies who are willing, and financially able to provide a gift (such as a gift card) for a certain amount of thank you notes received are leading the industry in ensuring there is a positive response for receiving thank-you's.

Here is an example of a recognition hierarchy:

The large awards are created to ensure the company is focused on stability and maintaining the culture. This why there are a few supreme awards dedicated to financials and values. The culture of a company is promoted from the top down, and employees should be able to see that whether they are an executive or a line level employee, they too have the ability to be honored with these awards. The next tier down is the of the year awards, which are created by department. This creates a culture of healthy competition to meet goals and be a MOLE. While these awards can be given to different individuals each year, depending on how they are doing at performance and meeting goals, it is possible one person can receive the award multiple times. That is okay as it supports growth and continued high performance.

Working down the pyramid, managers and employees should be giving and receiving certificates for their work every few months. These are created and given each time an employee does something worth telling a story about. It does not have to be an out of the world story, rather, something others should hear about how the individual made their life easier by doing their day-to-day role. This could be following up on an important issue until resolution or taking a project off someone else's desk who was feeling a bit overwhelmed. Again, certificates should be given from employee to employee at any level every couple months. They are delivered in front of peers and supervisors to let them know how much the values they exhibit are appreciated.

If managers and employees are buying in to the recognition culture, the next thing managers must monitor is how much recognition the MOLE employees are receiving. What you may notice is MOLE employees who have bought into the culture are sending these notes but are not receiving any in return. Is it due to their work performance or are there a group of employees who have not adopted the culture, which could decrease the MOLE employee's motivation?

Consider the case of an employee who was quite good at her job, but during her three-month coaching session she stated she had received no thank-you notes for anything she had done over the prior three months. When asked how many thank-you notes she gave, she said, "Well, I didn't give any." What had happened was, in not giving thank-you notes, the people that worked with her and around her began to believe she did not appreciate their work. Consequently, they did not give her thank-you notes. At the end of the coaching session we discussed the number of thank-you notes at some length and we strongly recommended she set aside a few minutes each Friday to choose at least one person to thank for special things they did for her during the week. She began this process, and by the next coaching session had given and received multiple thank-you notes. The main effect of all of this was her 360 survey, which measured how she fit into the culture of the company was markedly improved at the end of the year. Overall, always advise your team to give thank-you notes.

Ideally the entire staff are MOLE employees, but that is typically not the case in most organizations and special consideration needs to be focused on those who are making lives easier and not receiving anything different than those employees who are just getting by and enjoying their thank you notes. An example of a good thank you note is shown earlier in this chapter.

Organizations should be proud of the culture they are supporting and maintaining. Adding "Of the Year" awards or awards that promote company stability and longevity only increases an employee's ability to win an award and feel included. Recognition programs should inspire employees to become engaged and strive to achieve company goals. Effective recognition should also help reduce turnover and enhance business results.

There is no one-size-fits-all program for recognition, but it is impactful to do something to make MOLE employees feel like they are valued. This builds loyalty through recognition and work ethic through encouraging repeat behaviors. Recognition may also open the lines of communication between managers and employees. Employees who feel valued by their managers may be more open to discussing issues and sharing ideas with them, to the benefit of the department. Trust may be built when credit for success is shared. Managers play a key role in developing the culture of an organization. It is up to you, as the manager, to help create and develop the culture as the organization grows and more experts are mentored.

Recognition Jealousy

If you have ever tried to thank someone for doing something or recognize anyone in public, then you have most likely experienced the "damned if you do, damned if you don't" idiom. This is where you go out of your way to thank someone and then anyone else who has been involved, no matter how small their involvement has been, becomes upset, jealous, or downright mad they were not recognized as well.

You can almost guarantee this will happen if you have a monetary value on the award or if it is done at a large ceremony. This is common human nature, and as a MOLE leader it should not affect your ability to thank the people who deserve it. Others may need different recognition or none at all. We do, however, discourage anyone from recognizing teams of people. When an entire team is brought up, it is guaranteed one person did more work than the others, and disruption within the team occurs. If each person deserves to be recognized, find out what they actually did and thank them for that specific thing.

In one example of recognition jealousy, we had a manager who was frustrated with our insurance brokers. Meeting after meeting, the brokers were not fighting to get insurance rates down for staff, and each time the manager would push for more support from the brokers. Finally, the manager talked to her supervisor about considering a broker change. The manager was approved to begin comparisons, and because we have a larger human resources department, started by asking human resources staff for positive experiences with their former brokers at past organizations. This allowed the manager to understand the service they could be receiving from a new broker.

One employee shared glowing reviews about a former broker and the manager asked the person to reach out to their contact with a hope of moving forward to consideration. Because this employee had the relationship, the employee did a lot of the work, but the manager had the idea and set all the approvals throughout the process. The employee would not have done this had it not been for the manager initiating it. However, when the new broker saved the company thousands of dollars and lowered the cost of the benefit increase for staff, the employee no longer thought of the work as a team, and instead wanted to win the financial PIG award for herself. The manager was the one up for the award due to it being her idea and her initiative, not the employee.

The company pushed forward recognizing the manager and addressing the misunderstanding with the employee. The employee should be recognized through a thank-you or certificate, but it was not their initiative. They did as directed. They were not eligible for an award built on efficiencies. Moving forward, the communication for projects was to change into a "who started it" mindset. This may help your organization as well.

When a new idea comes out, discuss who started it. Whose idea is it, who is leading it, and who is helping. That way, later, when money or accolades are involved, no one is confused or emotionally involved about who should be receiving the recognition. Adjusting this process has saved us some emotional responses.

On more day-to-day recognition jealousy, MOLE leaders should stand behind their recognition. Recognize each employee for things they do, do not have preferential treatment, and try to find special things each individual does in order to make them feel supported and confident in their abilities. This should reduce the time they spend vocalizing frustration about the positive work for which others are receiving recognition.

Chapter Pearls

- Do not make jokes during recognition
- Recognize the value employees bring to the company
- Make recognition accessible and appropriate
- Recognize your own PIG and PIC winners
- Do not recognize teams

| 16 |

Compensating the MOLE

"You can't buy loyalty."
- Dr. Norman Johnson

As a MOLE leader in your company, you want all your staff to be happy and focused in their work. It is important the company work to develop a powerful reputation that attracts people to their organization.

Years ago, Dr. Johnson was living in Peoria, Illinois where Caterpillar Inc. has a large presence. They were known as "big yellow" and many people in the area worked for them. One day, Dr. Johnson got into a discussion with a man who worked as a bus driver for Caterpillar. He was full time and had to work odd hours transporting people to and from different locations. He spoke so highly of Caterpillar and was proud to be part of that larger network. Dr. Johnson could tell this man had high professionalism and commitment to his job; a real MOLE employee. Building a brand and a team that is proud of their employer is something for which we should all strive.

Because MOLEs are so important in your company and for you personally to make your life easier, it is critical they receive all the things they need from their career and job. If you will refer to chapter 1 for a moment and the discussion on the six areas of life that must be organized to be happy, you can see most of these areas can be directly related to work. The question becomes how does this MOLE view each of the six areas of life, and how do they view the company in relationship to their own particular needs in the six areas?

Health - Thumb

If you consider health for a moment, we said having a personal health plan was important for all people including a MOLE. The question is, how does the company and the office or workspace impact the MOLE's health? Is it a smoke-free area? Is there adequate paid time off so the person can take vacations and time off when needed? Is there flexibility in their schedule so they do not feel stressed? Is the amount of work that has to be accomplished achievable, or is it in fact very stressful to the individual? What support systems have been built in to the employee's job to ensure they do not take too much on themselves without assistance?

Personal Philosophy/Spirituality - Pointer

Is the business philosophy of the company matched to the personal philosophy of the MOLE? To answer this question, you have to get to know the MOLE very well. You must understand what motivates them, their long-term goals, and how they intend to lead their lives. In a company where every penny matters, if an employee must travel, they may stay in the cheapest hotels, eat the cheapest food, and travel by the cheapest conveyance. That may match well with some people's personal philosophy but not with others, where it could be viewed as greedy and tightfisted. Does the philosophic plan for growth in the company and growth in the individual match? Does the company's philosophy on education match with the individual's, or is it inadequate or too aggressive?

Environment - Middle

The third area to consider is environment. Does the work environment match the environment in which the MOLE is comfortable? For example, businesses frequently have pressure to dress in a very casual way. We had an opportunity to talk to a young person who was discussing a company that was a "great place to work" because you could wear your pajamas to work. The problem is many people would find such a dress down policy somewhat offensive, believing sloppy dress leads to sloppy work. The question is how does your MOLE feel about it? Is the environment in which they work clean, well-organized, and non-stressful?

Many years ago, Dr. Johnson worked in a factory that allowed the machine operators to decorate their machines any way they wanted to make more pleasant surroundings rather than the steel gray color you see in so many machine tools. The effect was dramatic. While at times the factory floor looked a little bizarre, the individual satisfaction ratings went up, meaning the individuals felt they had more control over their environment and workspace.

Money - Ring

The next area to consider is money. It is frequently said people hire into a company for money, but very quickly make a decision to stay or leave based upon all of the other aspects of the job. We think this is true, however money is important, and MOLEs must be adequately paid. You can't take advantage of people just because of loyalty or tenure. What is adequate is up to you and the MOLE with whom you are working. There are general pay scales and ranges you can look up very quickly on sites such as Salary.com and Glassdoor.com.

We recommend reviewing everybody's salary on January 1st, which is the same time we usually reevaluate all our clients. Usually cost of living increases run anywhere from 1.75 to 2.5 percent per year. Those are the numbers we usually consider for an increase for someone who had the same skillset a year ago they had today and is continuing to do a good job. It is in our best interest, however, to pay more money to those people that are more valuable or that have demonstrated new skills over the last year. As a leader, you will be involved in these discussions for the people reporting to you.

When a new employee joins your company, they have no knowledge of the company culture, little knowledge of the company's product lines, and the overall expectations of their job. By the following year they will be worth more money because they have been with you for a year. The year following that, they may become a senior level employee who will be worth more money again. From that point on, all of their raises should be related to cost of living and their professional growth as far as their skillset and new knowledge they have in the company. This requires you as a leader to monitor them closely, coach them constantly, and document formal meetings that include growth, professionalism, and skillset. All of this should be matched to the company's values and done in a format of professional strategic planning.

Our recommendation is MOLEs should be paid at least in the upper 10 percent of the pay scale in your area, and receive other perks such as 401(k), bonuses, and such things as frequent flyer miles and hotel points they can use personally. To repeat, MOLEs are not all about the money, but the money is very important.

Career/Work - Pinky

The next area is career/work. For a MOLE this may vary from a person who wants to continue to build their education and climb up the corporate ladder, to a person that just wants a guaranteed position for the next ten years before retirement. Once again, you have to know your staff personally and what drives them in order to help them reach their personal goals with this career. Does your company have an ongoing plan for professional development that might help a young person attend college part time or take other courses that would expand their skillset? Does your company offer a scholarship program they could access? Does this position allow them the personal satisfaction of accomplishment because they have the freedom of decision-making and the freedom to design their own workspace and area?

Love - Palm

The last of the six areas of life to consider is love. In the workplace this usually means solid friendships and respect for the people with whom you work. While the employer will have very little impact on the personal friendships developed by the MOLE, it is clear to us if people build bonded relationships with their friends at work, there is less tendency to want to leave them and go to another company.

When considering the compensation package for a MOLE or any employee, it is critical you think about all of the areas that are vital to individual's happiness. Another challenge you may face has to do with remote work. There is a population of individuals who thrive in an isolated environment, cut off from the office interactions. However, there continues to be articles discussing the challenges of some feeling left out of conversations or passed over for promotions. We tend to believe this occurs when one of two things have happened. First, to do less work and be home more. They log in to do just what they need to and then log off. This eliminates the informal talks or chats that they would have had in the office.. Second, it occurs when a company does not have a system to prevent a breakdown in relationships. In this case, if employees work from home and they do not have opportunities to discuss their work product, talk about future company growth or meet their team (even virtually), that is a company systems issue.

One of the tools we have used in our company to build relationships between employees is called "The Fluid and Electrolytes Meeting." When Dr. Johnson was a senior resident in training at a large Midwestern hospital, the workload was enormous and the days were long, sometimes stretching past 24 hours straight. There was no formal way for the residents to get together socially, as the hospital administrators would not allow residents to have time off for beer and snacks to socialize and decompress. They thought this was simply wasted time. He spoke to a number of pharmaceutical representatives who wanted to have more contact with the residents; they wanted to talk about their products and their medications. They were more than happy to supply beer, soft drinks, and snacks from potato chips to cheese trays. He called these meetings "Fluid and Electrolyte Conferences." They announced it over the hospital loudspeaker. Administration had no problems with the residents going to another conference, so it was never questioned. This system worked so well that as they continued to grow in size at the corporate office, they created a Fluid and Electrolyte Meeting every Friday at 4:30 p.m. This was at the end of the week, people's work was pretty much wrapped up by that time, and for 30 minutes they could have soft drinks, popcorn, or other snacks. The rules were you did not talk about work, you talked about what you were going to do over the weekend, how your family was doing, or discussed the latest movie. This is a social event people really enjoy. The Fluid and Electrolytes Meeting is simply an idea of how you can create a social networking program within your company. We no longer supply beer, as we believe this is generally a bad idea for multiple legal reasons, but certainly soft drinks and snacks work well.

It goes without saying you need to pay an adequate amount of cash and benefits, but do not lose track of all of the other areas from the health environment, the amount of physical work they have to do, the employee's personal philosophy versus the company's, the overall environment in which the people are working, career tracks for those that want it, and a comfortable long-term plan for those who are satisfied with their present positions. While you will have little input into the friendships developed with your staff, you can help foster those friendships by hosting company picnics and nights out at the ballgame where people can interact away from the work environment. Consider all of these aspects as you look at compensating the MOLEs that work for you. Always focus on the issue that these people are making your life easier. It is your job to make their life easier.

Chapter Pearls

- Consider your employee's six gardens of life
- Pay MOLEs in the top 10 percent

| 17 |

Tools, Tips, and Techniques for the MOLE Leader

Stories and Conversations that Teach and Guide

One of the great teaching tools MOLE leaders can use to guide their teams are common stories that demonstrate specific examples of behavior or concepts they wish to get across. As you have read the material in this book, you have come across many of these stories. For example, the slack in the screw, zombie ants, two women sitting at a bus stop, and the case of the midnight stalker.

We had a problem trying to describe to our senior staff in ways they could quickly understand whether a particular plan or action of theirs was helping or hurting the bottom line. Once we developed the story of the PIG, they all seemed to understand it immediately. The story of the PIG is based upon the movie and book *2001: A Space Odyssey* by Arthur C. Clarke (the film was directed by Stanley Kubrick).

There are a few variations between the movie and the book, and we have taken a few liberties with this story. It goes like this. At the dawn of mankind there was a small group of humanoids led by an individual by the name of Moon Watcher because he liked to look at the moon. These are really pre-humans; they are not even hunter-gatherers. They are just gatherers, and the problem is there was a lot of competition between all of the other critters that live in this area including hoofed animals, pigs, and even leopards. The little group is actually dying; they are starving. There is not enough nourishment eating the roots, berries, and bugs they find to keep the group alive. One day as the group is out searching for anything they can find to eat, they come across something unusual—a large slab that appears to be polished stone. It clearly is not natural, and it scares them because it is unclear from where it came.

In the story we learn this is a monolith sent to earth to evaluate and assist potential intelligence of organisms. As Moon Watcher and his little band become braver, they move closer and finally touch the monolith. When this happens, the monolith alters their DNA so for the first time they can begin to think strategically. This is something the little group has been unable to do their entire lives, they never had a desire other than to find something to eat, and they have never had long-term strategic ideas. A few days after this as Moon Watcher is out with this band searching for food, he has a thought. Wouldn't it be nice to sit in the cave where he is safe and to be completely full and satiated for the first time? Moon Watcher doesn't know how he's going to achieve this, and at this moment he has no particular plan, but he can see this image in his mind. A few more days go by, and Moon Watcher is trying to pull a root out of the ground he believes he can eat and a pig next to him is going after the same root. They are struggling back and forth. It occurs to Moon Watcher he could pick up a jawbone lying next to him and kill the pig and eat it. He grabs the jawbone, strikes the pig hard, and the pig goes down. All the other members of Moon Watcher's band immediately see what's going on and come over and continue beating the pig with clubs and rocks until they kill the pig. It is a big pig, but the vision was they were sitting in their cave eating and satiated. That means they have to get the pig to the cave. Moon Watcher grabs the pig because he has a clear vision in his mind of what to do and begins pulling the pig in that direction. Everybody is very excited and they all want to help. Some pull toward the cave, some don't quite have the idea and pull sideways, and some are pulling backwards. It is a tremendous tug of war, but eventually there are enough people understanding which direction they are going that Moon Watcher is able to get the pig to the cave. After all, there are leopards out there. The last scene of this part of the movie is Moon Watcher safe in his cave and satiated, for the first time no longer hungry.

At this point we suggested to our staff that Moon Watcher had a vision. We have a vision statement. Moon Watcher had a mission, pull the pig to the cave. We have a mission statement. The question is, which way are you pulling the pig? Are you pulling with me, or are you pulling sideways or against me? For every decision you have to make in business you must understand which direction it's going to pull the PIG—the Particularly Important Goal. This goal is always financial. When you want to hire a new employee to make life easier for your employees, which way will that pull the PIG? Will it allow you to get more contracts that are for this part of your growth of infrastructure and it's well worth it? On the other hand, if it will not help increase the bottom line, then it's pulling the PIG in the wrong direction. Always consider the PIG in all of your business decisions.

As you think about the training situations and concepts you need to get across to your team, if you can create a story that is memorable that will stay with them and demonstrate the important concept you will have achieved the goal.

360 Surveys

In our company, a 360 survey is an evaluation form that is filled out asking each person how the individual they are evaluating rates from the standpoint of each of our values. For example, the statement may be "This person demonstrates integrity." The rater then enters a number from 1 to 7 for each value. 1 is the lowest, and 7 the highest. There is usually between seven to fifteen people who evaluate each of the leaders of our company. This gives us a very solid view of the cultural fit and the reputation of the individual.

The rating scale is included in this section. You can choose a 1-5 scale or a 1-7 scale for your staff to use, just keep it consistent year over year. We prefer the 1-7 scale because it gives reviewers more leeway to score up and down without being extreme. Employees are trained that a 4 is barely meeting position expectations. This is someone who comes in and does exactly what is expected; no more, no less. They are fine, but not making your life any easier. We would prefer they would improve a little on that particular value. If they are a 2 or a 3, this is on the low end of the scale and a red flag. A 7 is rare and occurs based on a habit of identifying issues, recommending solutions, and following through. We expect staff to generally be in a 5-6 range. When we look at the individual scores, we like people to fall around a 5 average overall on the 1-7 scale.

By the time we have seven to fifteen people evaluating 25 different aspects of a leader's personality, we have a good overall view of how that person ranks in the company. It is important to understand that the 360 may not necessarily be a true evaluation of performance, but it is an accurate perception of the opinion people have about this person and their fit in the culture.

360 surveys are a common tool. They are a series of questionnaires given to people who work at your level, above you, or below you, so a generalized opinion of how you are functioning comes from people all around you. It generally takes at least seven or more opinions to be statistically accurate. The questions present the general opinion of your reputation in the company, and this defines how you fit into the culture of a company. Our internal numbers indicate if you fall in the bottom 10 percent of our 360 surveys there is a 50-75 percent chance you will leave the company either on your own accord or be removed within the next 12-month period.

The way we use the 360 is to look at our value system. We mentioned earlier we have 20+ core values. Each core value will have one or two statements specific to that core value. Each value's statement is framed to say something to the effect of, the employee is "VALUE DEFINITION." So for accountability, it would say, "The employee is accountable for their behavior and actions." At the end of the 360 when all the numbers are tabulated, we will be able to look at what your overall score is using our standard 1-7 scoring system. The key below explains ratings in more detail. At the end, each reviewer is also asked the key question, "Does this person make your life easier?" We can look at each value to see which values people believe you are the highest in and which values you are the lowest. It is important to remember this is an opinion survey and may not represent the entire truth, but that does not mean it is completely inaccurate. It does represent what people believe about you, and that is important. As you look at a 360 survey you can see how each statement is developed around a core value.

Once the 360 is completed the numbers are put on a large spreadsheet which ranks the individual against everyone who had 360s in the company. This is what tells us if you are in the top or bottom seventh of the company, and in which direction you are moving. Occasionally over a period of two or three years we can see a person moving slowly up or down in their reputation in the company. These can be key indicators of rising leaders or trouble brewing. If a person is ranked a 7 on a particular item, it is important to know why an individual thought this person was so good. We ask them to add a brief note concerning that score. If they are below a 4, we ask that they write a brief note so we can see what the problem areas are.

An example of the power of the 360 was an employee named Mary. Mary had been with the company for years, was a key person frequently ranked between 6 and 7 on the 360, and was a leader and trainer in the company. Everyone respected her. Then when the next 360 came out, Mary dropped to a 5. This was surprising, but not a bad score as she was in the top half of the company. There was nothing to indicate specifically what the problem was, her scores were simply lower. The following year she dropped to a 3. This was significant, and we began to notice that people said she lacked integrity, was not always truthful, and they could not trust her. We had known this employee for a long time and knew she was of the highest integrity, but there were times when she would give answers to questions very quickly, too quickly. In fact, she would give answers when she may not have been absolutely certain they were true. She was in fact guessing at the answer because she didn't know. She did not want to appear as if she didn't know because she was a "leader" in the company. We talked to her about this practice of answering before she knew the answer. She agreed and worked on it. Over the next year she was able to raise her score back up to a 5. The following year she dropped to a 2, and then to a 1. She was in the bottom 10 percent of the company. Once again, the same problems had arisen. We focused intensely on getting her to answer slowly, and in committee meetings everybody understood there were times she would answer too quick. If a question came up and she would blurt out an answer, we would stop and question her. "How do you know that, Mary? Are you sure about it?" She would then generally back up and say she would need to look into it to be absolutely certain. Her score improved from the bottom 10 percent back up to a 4. This decline over a number of years was very significant, and it was something we had not reacted to quickly enough. Consequently, her reputation was damaged and people could no longer work with her as a trusted team member. As you look at the patterns of people's scores on the 360, major changes in one direction or the other clearly are important.

In some instances you will have employees who consistently rank in the lower categories. With one employee I'm thinking of, her desk was always perfect. She was organized and precise. She showed up a few minutes early each day and stayed a bit later. She seemed fine but her 360 was bad indicating she was rude and did not interact. When we brought this to her attention, she agreed she does not choose to interact at work. She wants to come and do her job and the rank or perception did not bother her. This analysis with her allowed us to agree, as a group, that she would likely be in this category long-term but as long as she was not mean and her job performance was good, it was not an issue we needed to address or modify.

MOLE leaders also have to review 360 results with an eye on constructive feedback. Because 360s are anonymous, there will be people who are frustrated and want to be mean. In one instance, we had people writing derogatory terms or phrases like "Can't speak English well" on a foreign employees' survey. This is unhelpful, inappropriate, and should not be tolerated. Therefore, we recommend removing these comments before they ever are given to the employee. We want people to read the results to either reinforce the good efforts they are showing or consider adjusting their behavior as a way of growing from the constructive feedback. Another example of a response we removed was "Dresses within the dress code but is too trendy." This is unhelpful and unnecessary. There was no point to bring this to the employee's attention. People can dress as they like as long as it is acceptable within our policy, so it was removed and not another moment was wasted on the distracting, nonconstructive feedback. You don't want people walking out of these meetings crying.

Another example was Bill. Bill was hired in at a high level in the company and had a work history of leadership and success that went back over 20 years. His history was always in large companies or government organizations, and he had never been evaluated using a 360. The problem with Bill, which we identified fairly early, was that he was an elitist—he thought he was smarter than everybody else and he let everyone know it. He truly did not wish to be questioned. He also was given to viral conversations and would talk ill of other people in the company, not to help them but to tear them down. Bill was one of those individuals who thought he made himself look better by making everyone else look worse. We saw this coming for some time because the 360 was six months away, and we began to counsel him at length about it. He did not take well to it and suggested he had never received a bad review in his life and didn't expect one at this time. We were very specific about the problems and how he needed to change, otherwise we could end up with a bad result. Bill said, "We would have to agree to disagree." The day the 360 came out, Bill set a new record in the company—no one had ever scored as low as he did. He was shocked, and we were disappointed because we had invested a lot in him. His scores were so bad it was clear no one could work with him, and Bill had to be demoted and then replaced.

This is because we were unable to get through to Bill. He was the wrong culture fit for the company and saw no purpose in changing. His low values were largely discounted by him as a non-issue, because he had other areas of his work life he found more valuable. When you run in to this, it is okay. Just make sure to document the specific concerns and issues as much as you can. Focus on the job tasks not being accomplished because of the mismatched culture focus. Are they unable to collaborate, are people avoiding them because of the behaviors, what is the real root issue creating the problem on the 360? Very quickly you will learn if Bill is a MOLE employee who wants to acknowledge and improve, or if Bill disagrees and is not the correct fit. Bill is probably very successful wherever he ended up, but fortunately for our staff and culture, he is no longer with our organization. Properly designed and used, the 360 will be one of the most powerful instruments to evaluate people in your company.

Monkeys on Your Back

In 1974, Harvard Business Review published a report on metaphorical monkeys on your back by William Oncken, Jr., meaning someone has transferred a burden to you inappropriately. A leader is not a doer. You don't do your staff's work for them. When you bring a solution with a problem, you're not dumping monkeys on people's backs. When a team member brings a problem to you, don't let them simply dump the problem on you. Don't let them dump a monkey on your back. There are a number of reasons you should not accept these problems. First, it will make your life more complicated and difficult. They need to resolve their own issues. The second reason is you need to train your staff to bring a solution with the problem. This will help them get stronger and become better leaders. The day will come when you will need to identify someone who works for you as a potential leader in the company. If you have been training your staff to bring a solution with the problem, you will be ahead of the curve when this happens. Do not accept work your staff should be doing.

Over the years, we have been able to hire a number of employees with low employment experience. These are very bright young people who because of their age and experience have not had the opportunity to gain leadership skills. A similar version of this experience will happen with any new generation as it enters the workforce and has their own stigmatized behaviors and tendencies which may or may not be a true representation of them as an individual. Focus on character and the tasks assigned. Work closely with them to try to teach them to find a solution to the problems they are bringing to you. Try to teach them to never accept monkeys or dump monkeys on their supervisor's back. As you do this, these people became stronger and stronger.

Because of this internal system of teaching and encouraging people to bring solutions and not simply dumping problems onto someone else, we have been able to promote many of these inexperienced workers into senior leadership positions. We do not want leaders to spend their days finding solutions for their employees. As you think about your company and how people are handling their problems on a daily basis, always make sure you are not doing their work for them and they are getting stronger in their own leadership decision-making.

Systems Problems

When errors develop and people are repeatedly making errors, always step back and see if you have a "systems problem". For example, suppose you have an employee who is making multiple medication errors. When you research how medications are ordered and passed, you find medications are ordered by one person, unpacked and checked in by a second, set up for the pass by a third employee, and then someone else passes the medication about which they have no knowledge or understanding. Every time the medications are touched or ordered there is an opportunity for an error. There are too many steps and people involved. Therefore, you need to redesign the system to ensure those people who set up the medicines pass medicines. This will remove a major source of error. There may be other sources of system improvement, which will help reduce errors. Whatever the system is, when you see a pattern of errors, always look at the system to see if this is what is wrong, not the individual.

The MOLE Approach to Running a Meeting

Appropriate meetings are very important and vital to the function of the company. When you run a meeting, be sure everyone is prepared to work toward the purpose or vision of the meeting. Ensure your agenda addresses all of the issues for which it is responsible. Choose only those participants who have a direct role and responsibility for either reporting or gathering specific information. As you will recall, we do not want people to come as a meeting tourist, someone who comes to be entertained, but not to participate or learn anything new. Meetings are designed to move the company forward, to spread information, and to document your action items and goals are being completed in a timely manner. Typically, you should not allow texting or working on phones during a meeting. If someone needs to take a phone call, we recommend they get up and leave the room as to not disturb others. While you will have a scribe taking the meeting minutes, everybody should take notes so they do not have to be reminded of their particular action items. When the minutes from the meeting come out, be sure all of the attendees have reviewed the minutes in a timely matter and are working on the action items they were assigned. You will run into times when people will report on an action item they had from a week ago. The report may go something like this: "For action item 3, I was to call Joe. I called him today and he wasn't available, so I am unable to provide an update." What you notice is the action item was put off until the last minute, and they suddenly realized they hadn't accomplished their action item and then it was too late to get a response. Anytime a meeting attendee's response was they put in a call and are waiting for a response it is an indicator they waited too long to start the process, and this should be improved. As you review the action items from the prior week, always be sure you are looking to see who is and who is not completing them. Remember to inspect what you expect. Properly done business meetings can be the most powerful instrument you have to spread information and brainstorm.

You should not wait until the day of the meeting to start on action items on which you must report. Review the minutes as soon as they come out, and again three days prior to the next meeting to ensure your items will be complete and are up to date. Action items allow the attendees to inspect what they expect.

Exit Interview

Even if you do everything right with hiring, some people will still quit your organization. It is important not to take this emotionally or personally. There is a reason people leave organizations, and they are under no obligation to tell you why. Even if they give you a reason, there is no law that dictates the reason must be true. When a person quits their job (whether it be on the spot or by working out a notice), we recommend you conduct an exit interview.

The timing of the exit interview should be soon after the person leaves, but we do not recommend conducting it while they are still within the organization. It is recommended to conduct exit interviews when the person is no longer affiliated with the organization to relieve them of the burden of having to return back to work. If there are true issues going on and they want to share them, they are much more likely to share their critiques once they no longer have to explain themselves or defend their comments. Many employees today are conflict adverse. When their thoughts are challenged in this way, over an issue they want nothing to do with, their story can change and the grain of truth will be lost. You will not learn why they left by challenging them.

Quitting is uncomfortable. Consider this example when you read about the story of the earthworm in the Chapter 16; having to continue to confront the painful action they decided to make is less likely to illicit a truthful response. This is not to say the person was a bad employee if they did not tell the truth about why they were leaving. Being conflict adverse is common in the workplace. With a separation from employment and when there is no risk for retaliation, the former employee has no reason to withhold information on the reason they left. Employees want to be liked and supported. Former employees may care less about that.

Therefore, within a week after the employee exits the organization, we recommend human resources professional (not a manager of the employee) calls to conduct the exit interview. If they do not return the call, emailing will encourage a response. Calling is preferred to email in order to hear vocal inflections and to encourage elaboration of information.

When conducting an exit interview, having as many optional questions as possible will present the survey in the least confrontational way. If it's over the phone, the individual should be trained not to challenge the one-sided views of the person or to defend the organization. This is a one-sided listening and documentation exercise. Not everything the person says may be true, but not everything the person says may be false either. Many factors can contribute to why a person perceives an organization the way they do, and the goal of the exit interview is to try to identify where the perception is coming from, what the issue is, and how to avoid resignations in the future for the same reason.

It is preferable to hear people are leaving an organization to go back to school, because they are moving, or due to a medical issue preventing them from working. That means, in some respect, their decision is out of your control. It may even be out of the person's control themselves. These can be positive separations and the potential is left open to work together in the future if the situation arises.

It is not preferable to hear the manager or pay is the reason. When this comes up, there is work to be done by human resources and relevant managers. There may be pay comparisons that should be done, conversations with the manager to find out why they think the person left, and an audit of the manager's performance to gain a good understanding of why the individual cited them or the pay as their main point in leaving. Investigate until a solution is found or the information provided is deemed unsubstantiated. Each exit interview should be treated as a mini investigation and then the results should be posted as a metric for retention.

As you first start to track this information to create a retention metric, themes will begin to appear. Graphs may be created to show who is moving, who left for more money, and who left due to managers. As they start coming in, those themes should be reviewed and action items can be set. If five people in the past month left due to the same manager, what is the plan? If people in the same role are leaving due to pay, where are they going and who are you competing with for pay? Waste in the recruiting process will decrease when managers can start to see why people tend to leave, and they can intervene earlier by asking them how supervision or pay is going. Maybe even discussing the options of remote work if moving is a common concern. It is dependent on your organization and the tasks people need to perform. The goal is always to retain MOLE employees—though not retain everyone.

Typically exit interviews are only sent when an employee exits the organization, but we recommend they are sent when an employee exits any role resulting in reduced status. Therefore, if an employee changes from full time to part time, they get the survey. If an employee moves from part time to on-call, they get a survey. And if they leave the organization, they get a survey. We want to know why people are moving, what's shoving them to these changes in status.

Your exit or transition questions should focus on asking why they left (include categories once they start to become prevalent), determining if the person would come back to the job in the future, and if they felt they had all the tools they needed to do their job. At the end of the book, an example exit/transition survey is included. We suggest all of this be scored on a scale of 1-7. Whether verbal or in email form, we recommend pursuing comments and explanations for any scores of 1, 2 and/or 7. Reviewing exit and transition surveys is getting a glimpse into the thought process of employees and creates space for improvements and company reflection.

Chapter Pearls

- Coach employees at least quarterly
- Use stories to teach and guide

- Keep 360 evaluations constructive
- Review your systems (CAMPS-T)
- Do not accept monkeys
- Audit for systems problems
- Take a MOLE approach to meetings
- Conduct exit interviews

MOLD

| 18 |

People Who Make Our Lives Difficult

A MOLD employee is someone who **M**akes **O**ur **L**ives **D**ifficult. They will contact you with problems on an ongoing basis and do not think to bring a solution. Some of them will believe because they are not managers, they do not have to decide anything, they just do what they're told. This can be dangerous for an organization. MOLD does not take ownership and instead looks for whom to blame, rather than how to support and protect. To create a sustainable company, employees should be able to follow the expected procedures, continuously grow their knowledge to protect the company, and recommend more efficient or more appropriate changes as time goes on. Because of this, everyone needs a team of as many MOLEs as they can get. Every person has weaknesses, and humans are prone to make an occasional mistake. Therefore, we need to discuss what to do when an employee has continued to make repeated errors violating the company policy or culture. There are many books written on how to deal with difficult people and difficult employees. They usually revolve around looking deeply into why the person is difficult, trying to figure out what's motivating them, and somehow changing your behavior to accommodate them so in the end you can get the results from them you need. This is a lot of work. While we should always be fair with our staff, there comes a time when, if you are truly to make your life easier, MOLD must be removed.

The Three Reasons

A leader is a person who can get their staff to do the right thing at the right time in the right place. Why do we need leaders? Can't we just tell people what to do and have them do it? Unfortunately, the answer is no. In the end, there are only three reasons why people do not do the right thing:

1. You failed to give them the tools they needed.
2. You hired the wrong person.
3. They are lazy or a felon.

The first class of people who make errors is due to the fact you failed to give them the tools they needed to do their job. According to our internal company data, about 80 percent of the time, the leader did not give them the tools they needed to succeed. The most common tool is training. Staff take a lot more training and work than you realize, and nothing is intuitive. Many people will need to be retaught and reinforced on a regular basis, sometimes basic things like reminding a doctor to wash his hands between patients. One would think this would not be necessary, but it is.

Time

Time is another tool we may not have adequately provided. It is not uncommon we hire an employee and they are able to handle the work without difficulty. Then the work doubles in size and there is no increase in hours for the employee, so they are suddenly well beyond their ability to handle all of the work. Once again, it will be your duty as a leader to recognize this, assess the job duties, and redefine the job duties so the employee can accomplish everything expected.

We had a contract to provide health care to a small Midwestern client with an average daily detainee population of about 40. The contract called for a doctor to come in and hold a clinic once weekly, and for 20 hours of nursing time to be spread throughout five days. It was easy for the nurse to handle the work in the small jail, and we were able to identify and hire an excellent nurse who took personal responsibility for the facility and her patients. Over a period of time the average daily population grew to well over 100 detainees, and it was not possible for her to accomplish all of the work. She was very conscientious, worked very hard, and felt responsible to try to complete all of the work even though this was not possible. When reports came into the corporate office indicating the census was very high and she was falling behind in her work, the team was sent to the facility to analyze the problem and determine why the nurse was not accomplishing all of her work.

When it became abundantly clear the contract did not allow us to provide the hours necessary to get the work done, we talked to the client and advised him we needed to change the contract and increase the allotted time. The client reported to us the county commissioners would not allow any change in the contract, and if we demanded a change, they would put it out for bid and we may lose the contract. We talked to him about changing the job description of the nurse to remove certain duties like passing medications and performing chronic clinics, something we believe is important, but simply wasn't possible given the few hours we had. The sheriff agreed to this, but it was quickly clear even with these changes we were not getting the work done, and it was not in the best interest of our patients to allow this situation to continue. While neither we nor the client wanted to rebid the project with the possibility of losing the contract, it was clear this was in the best interest of our patients. We worked closely with the client to design an adequate program, which would function at the level of required quality. The bid was put out. Because of our prior experience, we were fortunate to retain the contract. However, even if we lost the contract, rebidding this project because we did not have enough hours to do the job correctly was the right thing to do. Always look at the workload of your staff to ensure it's possible for them to complete their jobs with the quality you require.

Tools

At other times, you may simply have not given someone adequate tools. Their computer may not work properly, they may need a printer, or it may be as simple as a blood pressure cuff or a stethoscope not working adequately.

It is correct to say all of the issues from this class of problems would be your fault. You should be doing the training, you should analyze the time, you should be sure the person has the adequate tools to do the job.

Bless Their Hearts

The second reason people do not perform is, for whatever reason, they simply cannot function. All of these issues would be your fault since you hired the wrong person. We see this in about 17 percent of our employees that are failing. This is a class two problem. These are the "bless their hearts" as coined in the professional sense by Mark Murphy. You like them a lot, but no matter how many times you tell them to lock their computer or get to work on time, something always comes up.

We just hired the wrong person. We refer to this as "a round peg in a square hole." An example is hiring Dr. Johnson to be your personal typist. Say he can type 15 words per minute (WPM). If he was hired as a professional typist with 15 WPM typing, he would not be able to perform at the level you would expect. This really would not be his fault, because he needed the job and he would accept the job because he does know how to type, but it would be the company's fault because they did not adequately test him to figure out if he was the right fit for the job. Another example is hiring people that cannot maintain the pace or cannot meet deadlines because, in their mind, the work is never perfect enough.

The bless your hearts are described as people who are very nice and they want to do well, but they are the wrong skillset for the job. It is the person you give a dictation to and they return it with multiple different fonts, font sizes, and incorrect letterhead. Or a person who answers the phone and doesn't screen a call right—ever. Annoyances grow and sometimes it is just easier to do the work yourself than wait a week for them to finish typing something at a 15 WPM rate.

While "bless their hearts" may be very nice and personable individuals, they will not help you accomplish the goals in the role, and may actually get you in to some legal or contractual issues with clients by not meeting agreed upon terms. When you come upon this situation, see if you have a position they may be able to handle—if not these people will have to be fired. We need to correct our error, but every case should be reviewed on its own and taken case by case.

Talented Terrors

Some people are extremely talented but are workplace bullies. We first learned about these individuals from Mark Murphy's book *Hiring for Attitude*. They have been coined "talented terrors" or "brilliant jerks." As we continue to research and learn about these workplace personalities, we hear various terms for the same overall concepts. For the purposes of this book, we will continue to call them "talented terrors," but in day-to-day life, these are the mean, angry people.

The talented terrors will tell you how wonderful they are, and they can be smarter and faster than anyone you've ever seen. They commonly start their sentences sharing how much experience they have in a subject area or telling you why they are so important. The problem evolves into a tendency for them to upset everyone with whom they come into contact, and consequently cause tension and trouble throughout the organization. They have their own ways to prove their success and will typically meet their goals, but no one will like them because the way they speak or present ideas is rude, unnecessarily direct, and discounts other's ideas (that may or may not also work). Over time, you will notice the lack of credit they give anyone else who assists them. Their attitudes are generally poor, and they do not care about having empathy or other's emotions.

As society starts to take notice of the way others are being treated, these are the individuals who may cause an organization to be brought a claim of hostility or harassment. They say whatever they want, and believe others need to shut their mouths and deal with it. They are mean—we cannot stress this enough. You're either with them or you're against them. In our experience, these individuals have a lot of anger within them and have no trouble expressing it outward. They do not see coaching as something they need, because they are already great.

There are only a few strategies we have for dealing with these personalities. First, the perception needs to be brought to their attention. Doing a 360 survey can help show the number of people who feel that way. Do not give them specific names of the people who reviewed them, though. The talented terrors will give excuses and yell at the people. It is useless to share the names of the reviewers, because it will not improve the behavior. Ask them what truth they see in the evaluations, and then give them very specific examples of times their attitude/behavior or task was not appropriate with the expectations.

When the time comes to separate them, work with human resources to make sure you have everything prepared. Through all of this you will have had ongoing conversations with the person to let them know adjustments you were making and things you were trying. This should not come as a surprise, but many times, both types will act like it is a shock. Talented terrors will look for someone to blame and say you do not respect hard workers. Bless your hearts will cry and say you lack loyalty. This is why trying to match people to the right job from the start is so important. No one wants to be in this situation.

Together this brings the number to 97 percent of all failures are the result of ineffective leadership, either through lack of training, monitoring, or hiring the wrong person.

Lazy/Felons

The third class of people who do not function is due to being lazy or a felon. We have found by internal data this accounts for about 3 percent of the reasons people do not function. The lazy people go to sleep on the night shift and continue to deflect their lack of productivity by shifting blame on any other individuals. Think of the individuals who will send a follow up email five minutes before a meeting, just so they can say they are waiting to hear back from you during the meeting.

The felons are individuals who break the law. They steal property, or in our industry, they steal narcotics. These are manipulators and unfortunately, some will get through.

When you run into a problem with an employee, you should take a step back and ask yourself which one of the three reasons that people do not function this person falls into. Remember 97 percent of the time either you did not train the person correctly or you hired the wrong person. This makes it your fault the person is not functioning.

Black and White Thinking vs. Empathy

It is not uncommon for new leaders to leap to the conclusion the employee is simply lazy or not willing to complete the task as directed. In other words, to this leader all employees are all good or all bad—black and white thinking. The proper approach is to step back with empathy and look for the gray. Walk through the three reasons people do not function. Almost invariably, you will figure out this is not a level three problem. Black and white thinking will create extreme problems with your leadership because you may be firing employees who are salvageable.

Once you have decided this is a level one, two, or three problem, the next question is to ask yourself what you could have done to prevent this problem from developing. If it is a level one problem, the answer will be to supply new equipment, do more training, and/or rewrite the job description so there isn't too much work for the individual.

If it is a class two problem, you simply hired the wrong person, and no amount of training has helped or is going to help. You do need to remove this person from your team. Unfortunately, it's not their fault, you simply put them in the wrong position. You need to be as kind a possible while you're helping them as they search for another job. In these cases, we generally recommend you do not try to prevent unemployment. We recommend you write a letter of recommendation for the good things they can do. The truth is they cannot stay with you because they cannot do the job.

If your decision is it is a level three problem and you need to move forward with discipline or termination, you still need to ask yourself what you could have done.

The Dweeb and the Tart

Some years ago, we had a contract to supply health care to a small Midwestern jail. The dweeb worked for us; he was a nurse. He was a bit awkward, overweight, and tended to lack certain social skills. One day, a tart was arrested for prostitution-related charges and was brought to jail. After she was there for a number of days, it occurred to her she would like to have some sleeping pills and maybe a better cell. She put in a sick call and talked to the dweeb to see what could be done. He informed her it was unlikely she was going to be given sleeping pills simply because she wanted them, because she had no medical diagnosis that required them. At this point, she suggested an illegal and immoral act in exchange for sleeping medication and a change of jail cells. The dweeb had the ability to change cells, as he carried keys to the cells to assign people, if necessary, to medical cells. The illegal act was consummated in the medical department, and the tart got her sleeping medication and a new cell. This arrangement continued until the tart realized she may have a "get out of jail free card." She went to the supervisor of the jail and suggested she had been raped, and now was suffering great stress. She would let all of that go if she was let out of jail. The jail supervisor called the dweeb at home and asked him to come in to discuss something—he wasn't specific. The dweeb knew he was in trouble. He came into the book in area of the jail carrying his suitcase, walked to the book-in officer and said, "I did it," indicating the illegal act, and prepared to be arrested. The supervisor came out immediately and suggested before he made any statements he needed to talk to an attorney. The dweeb was not deterred, and continued to proclaim the fact he was guilty, and an investigation began. The tart hired an attorney to sue to the jail and the dweeb. The case went on for years and finally culminated in a jury trial. The trial concluded with a decision, while the dweeb had done something illegal and immoral, the tart instigated the entire thing. At this time her claim was thrown out.

As we continued to review this case, we asked ourselves what could we do or could have done to prevent this. Clearly, it is hard to predict every way a person could violate the law. As we examined the case, the problem seemed to revolve around the nurse's ability to assign the prostitute a new cell. Had he not had this ability the whole thing may not have happened, as he would not have been able to offer this as enticement for the immoral act. At the time this occurred, we did not realize the jail had given him the ability to carry medical unit keys and assign patients. Following that case, we put out a rule throughout the entire company that nurses cannot carry cell keys for the purpose of reassigning detainees. While this is an extreme example, it does show if you think about these situations, it is very common you will be able to think of something you can do, if not now at least in the future, to prevent these things from happening again.

Unfortunately, cases like this can frequently damage the reputations of the employees and if not properly handled, even the company. In this case we had to fire the nurse and the department of registration removed his license. A bad outcome to a sad case.

Disciplining MOLD

From time to time it is necessary to discipline a class three employee. When we must, we discipline them for not demonstrating a particular core value. An example of this is a core value of positivity. It is important to demonstrate a positive outlook and attitude as you go about your daily work. When a person demonstrates a negative attitude and is negative to those around them, this must be corrected, therefore a discipline is written for not demonstrating the core value of positivity. The specific incidents or stories can be provided to show how the employee did not demonstrate the core value of positivity. Once again, it is important to refer your company's values before starting the process of corrective action or discipline.

The key point here is to correct and discipline people for the value they are not demonstrating, rather than the actual thing they did. You simply use their misbehavior as an example of not demonstrating the value. For example, years ago we had an employee that could simply not make it to work on time. Once she got to work she was a good employee, she knew her job, she could function at a high level, and we all enjoyed working with her. The problem was she didn't get to work until 15-25 minutes after the time she was supposed to be on the job. Her job, among other things, was to answer the phone, which meant if the phone rang at 8:05, someone had to pick up the extra work who may not have been fully trained to do this, and the system started to break down. She was late so often it became a big issue in our small office. We counseled her, worked with her, and finally decided we were not going to be able to get her to come in on time. We then made accommodations for her—instead of coming in at 8:00 a.m. she could come in at 8:30, and we would reassign the first 30 minutes of work to someone else, which put a big load on other people and caused some dissention in the office. At the time, we felt this was the lesser of evils. True to form, within a matter of a couple of weeks she couldn't make it to work at 8:30, and she would be 15-25 minutes late all the time. This was someone who simply could not look at a clock and tell what time she needed to leave for work. When we wrote her up for this problem, we did not write her up for being late. We wrote her up for not demonstrating the value of punctuality, which was a core value at that time. We used the details of her being late every day to demonstrate how she was not pursuing a value we had all agreed to. An example of this write up is below:

This example shows it is fair to employees to explain what happened. You do not need to hide behind fancy words or blame. You state the facts of the situation. You did not exhibit this value, we have tried unsuccessfully to help, so here is the expectation set for you moving forward. There is an inability to argue the facts of punctuality. Do not get caught up in the drama of why they were late, such as car breaking down, dog ran away, kid was sick, overslept, etc. The point is they were not punctual, and you need someone who is punctual. You then address their immediate action items for retraining so when they walk away from this coaching, they are retrained with all the information they need to understand the policies and expectations set for them.

When a MOLE employee makes a task error, they generally know it and have a plan to not let it happen again. MOLD employees can over explain and move on from the task error, undervaluing the underlying issue they caused with their behavior. MOLD employees can easily discount the value they failed to exhibit and view it instead, as unimportant.

When the issue is approached with the employee, they may undervalue their dependability and professionalism by notifying you of every other individual who has been late and not disciplined. The key point here is they are not denying their tardiness. However, the other individuals who may also be tardy are not the point you want to discuss. You want to make the person aware *they* are not exhibiting the expected value of dependability and professionalism, and the behavior needs immediate improvement. There is no arguing the fact. Furthermore, because MOLD employees may be smart and specific, it is necessary to document conversations and decisions.

Argument or not, there will be a response from the individual. This is the time when a MOLE leader will work on their ability to actively listen and keep their opinions to themselves. Know you have done everything you needed to in order to help this person, and this is the next appropriate and progressive step to helping them succeed. Do not respond with emotion or meet their level of frustration, embarrassment, etc. Instead respond with statements that encourage signing the form to acknowledge the conversation and starting fresh with this new understanding of expectations.

This is a hard skill to master, as humans want to defend when interacted with from a parent to child level. Refer back to the "I'm OK, You're OK" section in Chapter 2 for more information. Therefore, there is no need to defend other employees who lack accountability, because you surely are dealing with them confidentially and appropriately as well. You are an adult and choose to respond back to the adult-to-adult level. The control and focus for this interaction is to listen to what they are saying and what they are not saying.

Documentation is key with MOLD so no one leaves the room with a different understanding of the point of the conversation. As an example, we had conversations with a former employee who misinterpreted a counseling session aimed at modifying their behavior when dealing with difficult people, believing they were being told how to deal with people who are difficult. If a manager feels the issue is important enough to discuss, it is equally as important to ensure the documentation matches the conversation.

The intent of disciplining an employee is to immediately help them resolve the deficiency so it does not lead to separation from employment. The terms vary in organizations, but this type of intervention is typically called a write-up. For the purposes of separation, these documents support that managers did in fact tell the employee if they do not change their behavior, they will be terminated. Do not be afraid of paperwork.

Because discipline can create an atmosphere of conflict or defensiveness, the discipline process is not the most exciting part of the manager role. Some managers handle discipline more easily than others, and by doing so generally means they have experience and a comfort level with the process. Still, some individuals may have a more difficult time disciplining a coworker due to their own personality tendency to avoid conflict. Some managers think (in the moment) it is easier to ignore small behaviors and hope they go away. For example, if an angry employee is coming in to work five minutes late every day, the manager may not want to be confrontational and downplay the fact they are always five minutes late. But in the greater scheme of things, the five minutes is disrespectful to the organization and to the manager. Not addressing the situation does not help when later the employee starts setting their own schedule without asking. If you do not correct the behavior early, it may be impossible to correct without separation from employment.

Telling an employee they are deficient and need to improve is not typically any easy conversation to have, but it should not come as a shock to the individual. Because of this, it is important these types of discussions do not get delayed for a later date. A manager should remain professional and be courteous to the employee, regardless of his or her reaction. Following the interaction, the employee should be able to state what was deficient and know the correct behavior expectations.

Before drafting the documentation, it is a good opportunity to consult with a human resources department, consultant, or anyone specialized in handling employee issues. Early intervention, discussions, and documentation is extremely helpful to ensure everyone is on the same page as it relates to a task or behavior being adjusted. Whether or not you choose to seek consultation, ask yourself, "Have I given them all the training and tools they need to be successful?" If no, consider getting a plan to get them the training or tools they need to be successful. Then ask yourself what policy or value the person's behavior violated. Finally, determine if there is something more you could reasonably do to help this person succeed.

Document the date, situation, policy violations, and corrective action to be taken on a form so it is clear. Prior to scheduling a meeting with the employee regarding the discipline, it is good practice to ask the employee about the situation to get their perspective. The manager should leave the conversation with a statement such as, "I will finish reviewing the situation and then we'll meet again." At times, the employee will have a new perspective that totally explains the situation and does not actually create a violation.

After drafting the conference and communicating with the employee, consulting with a human resources professional will allow a manager to get a third-party perspective. It will also assist with a review of any liability the manager could be opening themselves up to based upon how the document is drafted.

Ideally, the meeting should be scheduled face-to-face with the employee, but it will depend on the type of organization in which you work. As a general rule, it is not advised to postpone for a "right time" at a later date. Depending in the circumstances, it may be appropriate to wait until the end of a shift or for a specific moment, but this should be reviewed to ensure the reason is sound.

Depending on the nature of the conversation, the employee may become emotional. This does not typically occur with MOLE employees. These emotions could include anger, confusion, sadness, etc. The manager should be prepared for any of these. The goal is to notify the employee of the performance concern, retrain on the policies, and end the meeting. This meeting is not intended to be a conversation. At this point, the employee should have already had their side of the story listened to, and a good faith determination has been reached. Statements that may help are, "I understand you're upset" and "I understand you disagree."

Request the employee sign the form during the meeting to acknowledge the meeting; not necessarily to agree. Then, immediately train the employee on the corrective action so they leave the meeting understanding how they should modify their behavior to not violate the policy moving forward.

During the meeting, if the employee asks for a copy of the form, we recommend you allow them to have a copy if they first sign it. They are not entitled to a copy if they refuse to sign. Signing the form does not mean they necessarily agree with the information provided, but instead, signing the form is an acknowledgment of the discussion. If the employee does not ask for a copy during the meeting but later asks for one, consult with human resources. Each state has different requirements for what employees are allowed and not allowed to have copies of. Some employees are not entitled to any documentation a company has on them. If you bend the rules for one person, you can inadvertently be discriminating against others who do not obtain the documents as requested.

Do not fall for a trap of inappropriately boosting their ego with statements that are not factual, such as "You are such an asset" or similar statements that attempt to downplay the goals of the meeting. Additionally, do not make statements that their health or other similar trait is the company's upmost priority. The person is being disciplined for a specific reason, and this should be the focus. It does not mean they are deficient in any other area of their life, so speaking to anything other than the goal of the meeting is pointless. Making the meeting about anything other than their performance opens you up for lawsuits, and inappropriately gives the perception the discipline had something to do with their personal, medical, or other issues.

If the individual cites an inappropriate reason, immediately deny and restate the reason. As an example, if a female employee states, "You didn't write me up me because I broke the policy, you wrote me up me because I'm pregnant! It is illegal for you to write me up or fire me because I'm pregnant!" Do not get distracted or fearful of false allegations and claims. Respond, "No. That is not true. The reason I have written you up is…." This may help later if the employee makes a complaint against the manager. Threats and allegations of this nature may come up with other situations, too. As long as the manager is not discriminating or retaliating against an employee, there is no cause for concern for dealing with issues, and they can be handled and denied on the spot.

You may also end the meeting if it becomes unproductive. If you experience anger, do not raise your voice or argue facts. You already know the facts, or the discipline would not have occurred. Wait for them to finish talking and say, "The decision has been made and I am ending the discipline meeting at this time. Thank you." You have full control of the conversation—do not give it away by fighting.

Correcting a MOLE employee is typically a much more efficient situation. By the time the meeting occurs a MOLE employee has already thought about what they violated and developed a solution as to how it will not occur again. The personality aspects in a MOLE employee do not matter when it comes to discipline. No matter if they are more extroverted, more emotional, more perfectionistic—they understand the issue and do not want it to happen again. Managers will show up to a meeting prepared to deliver the form, and the MOLE employee typically acknowledges the situation, might apologize or give a short explanation, then signs all training documents. The meeting ends, and everyone moves forward with a little more knowledge as to the expectations of the organization. MOLE employees truly do make your life easier.

By way of example let's say an employee made a decision that cost the organization a large sum of money. In this situation, it will be assumed the employee did not immediately report the loss of funds, and instead the supervisor found out through regular business or through employee gossip. The supervisor should approach the employee and notify them they would like to meet regarding the loss of funds and schedule a time to meet. During the meeting the supervisor would initiate the conversation and ask what happened. A MOLE employee will immediately and honestly explain the facts of what occurred, apologize for the error, and make recommendations for how it will not occur in the future. They might even find a way to decrease the loss. There should not be much speaking from the supervisor other than to acknowledge the employee's error, thank them for accepting responsibility, and to conduct any remedial training to ensure expectations are met. A MOLE employee will understand they will need to sign documentation to confirm the situation occurred and what they are expected to do in their role, i.e., coaching form and policies.

A MOLD employee who makes your life difficult will use the time to blame others who were aware or involved, deflect blame, apologize *on behalf of* others, or apologize for making individuals *feel* a certain way—but will not actually apologize for their error that resulted in a loss of funds. These individuals will dramatically raise their voice, try to change the subject, and may even go as far as to refuse to sign the coaching forms to document they were spoken to because they "do not agree" with being disciplined for their error. Employees who behave this way will continue to escalate their behaviors and act out more until separation form employment. If it is on their terms, it will most likely be after several unsubstantiated complaints against co-workers.

Firing MOLD

If the organization decides to separate a MOLD employee, the phone lines may get very busy as the employee attempts to bully staff into overturning the separation or makes threats of lawsuits. Early intervention is key to avoid the emotionally hard post-hire process. Check the documentation you have on file regarding the issue, decide if termination is necessary, and check any laws or regulations in your state that may affect the ability to terminate an employee. This could be due to varying "at will" laws, employment contracts if your organization has them, or job protections as designated by law. Consult with an employee issue specialist, human resources, or an employment lawyer if you get confused as to what you need to do (terminate or not).

As a leader, you must deal with the small issues as they occur, document early, and try to overcome the manageable issues before the separation becomes negative. Delaying or avoiding uncomfortable conversations with employees is not effective and will only create a culture where you have accepted the behavior for so long, the employee doesn't believe they need ever change. Should you have a manager who wants to avoid uncomfortable conversations, it is important to have them work with human resources or get involved in a leadership training program about having difficult conversations.

In an extreme example if this, we had an employee who worked for the organization for many years. She was brought in for coaching numerous times and knew many of the leadership skills you have read about in this book. Specifically, we recall her learning about how to deal with difficult people when she was being told people found her leadership style to be "off with your head" for one error and condescending at their facility. She would walk in a new medical unit and tell everyone who she was and why what they were doing was wrong. Her clinical skills seemed to be excellent, but her people skills were continuously lacking. We brought her in to talk to her face-to-face numerous times and documented those interactions. Finally, she had been locked out of so many facilities due to her behavior we had to release her from employment. This was emotionally hard because we knew her, we had worked with her for so long, and we still could not help her to understand she needed to change her communication and behavior.

Once she left the organization, she filed for unemployment and then also filed an Equal Employment Opportunity Commission (EEOC) complaint claiming we fired her because of a discriminatory reason that was not performance based. This was emotionally hard to understand, because we had a long tenure together and a business friendship. While we were responding to the EEOC on the fact we did not terminate due to a discriminatory reason (through costly legal expenses), we also had to respond to the unemployment claim. Unemployment claims tend to be determined quickly. Within a month or so, we had a determination that we had "won" her unemployment claim, and she was not entitled to unemployment money. The EEOC is quite a different experience and operates through research and comparisons. Using what we received from the unemployment office helped us to prove the EEOC claim was invalid. It was a frivolous case and completely unfounded, but we spent a good amount of money proving our innocence. She, however, was not out any money at all.

This situation became an internal lesson to further push out the leadership training and ensure leaders in our organization start intervening early and calling out inappropriate behavior that may lead to separation from employment. Without our constant documentation, overcoming unemployment and the EEOC would have been more difficult. For those of you who have not defended an organization from an

EEOC compliant, the burden is on the employer to prove innocence, not necessarily on the employee to prove discrimination occurred. Failing to document and have conversations when issues start could result in post-hire arguments, which from your perspective are inaccurate, such as "I was never trained" or "I did everything they asked me to." Having proper documentation of trying to assist an employee to improve their behavior will assist managers in emotional separations and time-wasting frivolous lawsuits.

Chapter Pearls

- Determine the reason for MOLD (the three reasons)
- Understand strengths and weaknesses of Talented Terrors and "Bless Their Hearts"
- Provide action or discipline based on core values
- Train on black and white thinking vs. empathy
- Often times, lazy/felons cannot be changed (the nurse and the prostitute)
- Early intervention is important
- Do not underestimate the power of documentation

Closing

As we come to the close of this book, we ask you to reconsider the questions from the introduction: Is your life perfect? Why not? What have you done about it? Your answers to these questions may be starting to change as you learn a new way of thinking about leadership and the tools to apply.

Throughout this book we have reviewed some overarching sections of becoming, communicating, and executing as a MOLE leader. You learned to develop your own skills, communication, and execution techniques. You learned to identify other MOLEs in the workplace or develop them yourself through training, mentoring and coaching.

Finally, we expanded on how to build your own team of MOLE employees and continued to focus on the need to make lives easier. You need to avoid MOLD. Again, making lives easier is not about avoiding work or responsibility, it is about making the most of everything you do and becoming efficient at it. MOLEs are not perfect, but they speak up when they need help and take accountability so they may return to the path they were on. You have now learned a new way of thinking of personal productivity and leadership.

One of the major takeaways we would like readers to have is you are in control of your life. MOLE theory is all about you and your needs. You need air, food, water, and shelter to live, but to make your life easier you need to know what your personal goals are, because they are different for every person. The focused efforts you put in to reach your personal goals will result in your ability to reach those goals. The effort you put in, if not focused, will result in becoming burned out or simply overwhelmed. Help yourself first. Then help others around you to recognize their MOLE greatness.

Please use this book as a personal guide or roadmap to develop your skills. The entire purpose of the book was to give readers an opportunity to learn the MOLE Theory and give concrete tools to jump start your transition. We wish you the best in your future endeavors!

About the Authors

Norman Johnson, MD, FACP, ABAM, CCHP

Dr. Johnson, founder and Chairman of the Board of Advanced Correctional Healthcare, Inc., has over 40 years of experience in direct healthcare management. His background includes the establishment of a large medical group consisting of nine primary care physicians and eight subspecialties.

Dr. Johnson is board certified in internal medicine, certified by the American Board of Addiction Medicine (ABAM), and a member of the Society of Correctional Physicians. In November 2016, Dr. Johnson was recognized by the American College of Physicians as a Fellow. Fellowship in the American College of Physicians is a high honor, showing distinction from colleagues who recognize your accomplishments over and above the practice of medicine.

Dr. Johnson possesses extensive experience in the correctional healthcare environment, including facility analysis, program development, professional staffing, and contract negotiation. He is involved and provides educational programs for national, state, and county associations.

Angela Moriarity, PhD, SHRM-SCP, CCHP

Angela Moriarity, PhD, President of MOLE Theory, LLC, has almost two decades of experience in human resources with an emphasis on employee issues, coaching, and leadership development. She has conducted large scale organizational changes, including improving corporate culture, creating new interview processes to hire the right people, and taking on non-compliant processes to reestablish compliance on all levels.

Dr. Moriarity is a life-long learner. She holds a PhD in Business Management with a specialization in Human Resources where she completed a nation-wide study on organizational commitment and turnover intent. She holds a Master's Degree in Business Administration and a Bachelor's Degree in Psychology. Dr. Moriarity is senior certified professional with the Society for Human Resource Management (SHRM) and a certified correctional health professional (CCHP) by the National Commission on Correctional Healthcare. She has sat on a variety of community boards and as of 2024, recently changed career course to return to school with a plan to join the medical community.

Dr. Moriarity has been awarded HRO Today's 2017 Chief Human Resource Officer of the Year Leader of Distinction award, Peoria Chamber of Commerce's 2018 ATHENA Young Professional Award for Women in Leadership, and was a recipient of iBi Magazine's 2019 40 Leaders Under 40 award. In 2020, she was honored with the 25 Women in Leadership Award by the Peoria Chamber of Commerce & WEEK 25.

SUGGESTED READING LIST

Clifton, Jim, and Jim Hartner. *It's the Manager*. Washington, D.C.: Gallup Press, 2019.

Covey, Stephen M.R. *The Speed of Trust*. New York: Free Press, 2006.

Covey, Stephen M.R. *The 7 Habits of Highly Effective People*. New York: Simon & Schuster: 1989.

Goggins, David. *Can't Hurt Me*. Austin: Lioncrest, 2020.

Gostick, Adrian, and Chester Elton. *The Carrot Principle*. New York: Free Press, 2009.

Harris, Thomas A. *I'm OK—You're OK*. New York: Harper, 1969.

McChesney, Chris, Sean Covey, and Jim Huling. *The 4 Disciplines of Execution*. New York: Simon & Schuster, 2012.

Murphy, Mark. *Hard Goals*. New York: McGraw-Hill, 2010.

Murphy, Mark. *Hundred Percenters*. New York: McGraw-Hill, 2009.

Murphy, Mark. *Hiring for Attitude*. New York: McGraw-Hill, 2011.

Selk, Jason. *Executive Toughness*. New York: McGraw-Hill, 2011.

INDEX

A Message to Garcia	73
A Road Map to Success for the MOLE Leader	178
Action Items	63
Agreeing with a "Crazy Person"	81
Airline Attendant	8
Application	115
Assume Positive Intent	24
Behavioral Modification	135
Black and White Thinking vs. Empathy	240
Bless Their Hearts	236
Bright Shiny Things	83
Bring a Solution with the Problem	83
Building a Team	95
Business Networking	113
Cadence of Contacts	155
Cadence of Monitoring	175
CAMPS-T	159
Case of the Midnight Stalker	124
Certificates	199
Coaching Review Philosophy	158

Commitments	62
Company Core Values	187
Company Culture Review	104
Company Websites	113
Concept Penetration	142
Consistency in Training	148
Disciplining MOLD	242
Dweeb and the Tart	241
Earthworms	136
Email	31
Execution Score	66
Executive Search Firms	114
Exit Interview	226
Face-to-Face Communication	28
Firing MOLD	250
Gardens of Your Life	17
HARD Goals	192
Honest SWOT Analysis	183
How to Create Goals	190
Industry Specific Awards	201
Job Description Review	164
Lazy/Felons	239

Learning Management Systems and Large Meetings	40
Lectures	133
Liars	26
MAC Programs	147
Meetings	61
Meeting Tourists	62
Mini PIG	202
MOLE Interview	123
MOLE Approach to Running a Meeting	225
MOLEs Never Get Angry	70
MOLE Stress	21
MOLE Test	161
Monkeys on Your Back	223
Notebooks and Records	64
Of the Year Awards	201
Pass Information, Not Fear	49
Perfect Day	79
Personal MOLE Values	70
Personal Time Study by the MOLE	77
Phone Communication	30
PIG Award	202

Preliminary Hiring Factors	110
Professionalism Integrity Commitment (PIC) Award	203
Rabbit Holes	84
Recognition Jealousy	207
Remote Monitoring	174
Science of Degradation	172
Scorecards and Scoreboards	138
Seat Belt Concept: How to Maintain Composure	80
Second Level of Leadership/Team Leader	90
Six Areas of Life	10
Skill Interview	116
Slack in the Screw	145
Social Media	39
Solutions without Problems	86
Sourcing	112
Strategic Manual for Job Positions	167
Strategic Plan for Happiness	18
Strategic Plan Meetings	181
Systems Problems	224
Talented Terrors	237
Teaching	132

Texting	38
Third Level of Leadership/ Advanced MOLE Leadership	91
Three Reasons	233
Time	233
Tools	235
Training Timeline	131
Training Tourists	136
Transactional Analysis Theory	40
Trouble and the MOLE	69
Using Values	108
Values Review	106
Vampires	55
Video Communication/ Conferencing	29
Video Messages	30
Viral Conversations	50
Viral Thoughts	51
Visceral Training	137
Voicemail	31
What is a Mission	180
What is a Vision	179
Word of the Year	182

Work Ethic and the MOLE	72
You Inspect What You Expect	170
Zombies	54
2/4/6 Programs	64
11:00 Rule	59
12 Step Approach to Dealing with People	43
360 Surveys	218

www.ingramcontent.com/pod-product-compliance
Lightning Source LLC
LaVergne TN
LVHW010042290325
806893LV00007B/17